Center
Religi
4020 N....... Hall
Notre Dame, IN 46556

Giving
and
Stewardship in an
Effective
Church

Other books by Kennon L. Callahan

Giving and Stewardship in an Effective Church

A Guide for Every Member

Kennon L. Callahan

JOSSEY-BASS
A Wiley Imprint
www.josseybass.com

Published by Jossey-Bass
A Wiley Imprint
989 Market Street, San Francisco, CA 94103-1741   www.josseybass.com

FIRST JOSSEY-BASS EDITION PUBLISHED IN 1997. THIS BOOK WAS ORIGINALLY PUBLISHED BY HARPERSANFRANCISCO.

Jossey-Bass books and products are available through most bookstores. To contact Jossey-Bass directly call our Customer Care Department within the U.S. at 800-956-7739, outside the U.S. at 317-572-3986 or fax 317-572-4002.

Jossey-Bass also publishes its books in a variety of electronic formats. Some content that appears in print may not be available in electronic books.

Library of Congress Cataloging-in-Publication Data

Callahan, Kennon L.
    Giving and stewardship in an effective church : a guide for every member / Kennon L. Callahan.
        p.   cm.
    Originally published: San Francisco : HarperSanFrancisco, 1992
        ISBN 0-7879-3867-X (alk. paper)
    1. Christian giving.   2. Stewardship, Christian.   I. Title
[BV772.C353   1997]
248'.6—dc21   97-25584

HB Printing   10 9 8 7 6 5 4

To our sons, Ken and Mike, whose lives have enriched our lives.
We are grateful for their wisdom and spirit,
compassion and joy . . . for being family together.
                                Kennon and Julie Callahan

Contents

Preface

This book is about giving. It is for you and your whole congregation. Invite your congregation to read and discuss the book in study sessions or in a retreat setting.

This book shares wisdom and insights, principles and practical suggestions about giving. By implementing the ideas and suggestions in this book, your own giving and the giving of your congregation will grow.

I want to acknowledge and thank the following people for their influence in my life: Orville and Mary Hissom, Harold and Wilma Dodds, and Mrs. Ida Mae Stratton of Brady Lake Church; Gene and Ann St. Clair, Walter and Virginia Hoy, and Glen and Virginia Johnson of Lovers Lane Church; John and Katy Bush and John and Janet Gordon of Pleasant Valley Church; Richard and Elizabeth Warden of Reveille Church; and Ian and Joan Tanner and Dean and Sandra Drayton of the Uniting Church of Australia. These people, and many, many more, have taught me much about giving over the years. To all of them, I am deeply indebted.

Julia McCoy Callahan has been remarkable in her influence on my own life. Her valuable suggestions and direct contributions have strengthened this book immeasurably. It is an amazing experience to live and share together with her.

I especially want to thank John Shopp, senior editor at Harper San Francisco, for his major contributions to the publication of this book. His editorial wisdom and craftsmanship have been extraordinary. John and I have enjoyed a long, creative, and constructive relationship. Hilary Vartanian and Rosana Francescato of Harper San Francisco have made many excellent contributions to the book. It is a genuine joy to work with John, Hilary, Rosana, and the many gifted people at Harper San Francisco.

My thanks also to Dwayne Roberts, who typed the original manuscript as well as the revisions that followed. She has labored long and hard to help bring the book into being.

May the book help you in your living and your giving. God bless and be with you.

PART ONE

Giving Principles

Chapter 1

====================

Mission and Giving

Living is giving. This is the first principle for giving. We live life best as we give our strengths, gifts, and competencies in the service of God's mission. We are called to serve, not survive. Our giving makes a difference in our families, our work, our community, our world, and our church.

We want our lives to count. We want to make a difference. We do not want to spend and waste our lives in flimsy, foolish ways. We want the confidence that we are living for a cause that counts. Our lives count best when we direct them to the mission of God.

The mission of God is eternal. Civilizations rise and fall, empires come and go, new beginnings emerge—but the mission of God goes on forever. As the twenty-first century stretches before us, the possibilities for mission are extraordinary.

Mission is more important than money. This does not diminish, deprecate, nor deny the value of money. Money is important. It is a means by which a portion of God's mission is advanced. Gaining a constructive perspective invites understanding the relationship between mission and money. It is important to keep an appropriate balance between the two. And it is crucial to never let money become more important than mission.

A clear vision of mission will be decisive in fostering your congregation's capacity for giving. Two things are true of congregations:

- Congregations never have enough money.

- Congregations have all the money they really need for God's mission.

In mission congregations, there is never enough money. In growing congregations, there is never enough money. These congregations are always giving away more money than they have. They are always living at the edge of their resources.

Similarly, declining and dying congregations never have enough money either, but for an entirely different reason. These congregations have forgotten mission. People do not give generously to congregations that have allowed mission to recede into the background. When the focus of meeting after meeting is primarily on getting enough money to balance the budget, people's generous impulses wither.

God calls congregations to mission. Churches that become preoccupied with money have lost their way. They have lost their integrity by their narrow focus on money. Such congregations do just enough mission to delude themselves that they have not lost their way. But their central preoccupations are with money, membership, and maintenance.

Congregations with a vision of mission will have all the money they really need. Although it will seem as though there is not enough money, it nonetheless will be sufficient for the mission.

Money follows mission, not the reverse. This is a shorthand way of saying that the stronger the congregation's relational characteristics, the easier it is to raise money. The stronger the congregation's mission, visitation, worship, groupings, leadership, and decision making, the stronger the giving.

Of the twelve characteristics consistently present in effective congregations, six are relational (person-centered) characteristics and six are functional (organizational) characteristics, as can be seen in Table 1.1.

I often am invited to help congregations—some almost on the verge of bankruptcy—to develop more solid financial resources. Our first step is to see which relational characteristics are already strong. Second, we decide which relational characteristics can be added as new strengths. Third, we consider which functional characteristics will help. Finally, when these areas have been addressed, we focus on building solid financial resources. The stronger the relational characteristics, the easier it is to increase giving.

People will give more for mission than for maintenance. When you grow the mission, the money will come—and it will be sufficient for the mission.

We do the mission for the integrity of the mission. Mission is the goal in itself. The purpose of mission is not to acquire money. The

Relational	Functional
1. Specific, concrete missional objectives	7. Several competent programs and activities
2. Pastoral/lay visitation in the community	8. Open accessibility of church, leaders, and pastor
3. Corporate, dynamic worship	9. High visibility of church in community
4. Significant relational groupings	10. Adequate parking, land, and landscaping
5. Strong leadership resources	11. Adequate space and facilities
6. Solid, participatory decision making	12. Solid financial resources

Table 1.1

strength of the mission draws the money. The stronger the mission, the more people give.

This book is about giving and stewardship. Giving increases in direct proportion to the strength of the mission. Therefore, may your heart be in God's mission.

Where your treasure is, there will your heart be also.

Matt. 6:21

And where your heart is, there will be your treasure also.

Grow the mission. Grow the giving. Keep your focus on these two central objectives. Your life will be richer and fuller. The mission of your congregation will be stronger and more powerful.

Sometimes, people think the stumbling block to growing mission is money—or rather, the lack of money. Someone will inevitably say, "We can't do that; we don't have enough money." When congregations grow the mission, the giving comes. Grow your mission, and God will supply the money for the mission.

Sometimes a stumbling block can be people's natural hesitation and timidity about asking for money. They are uncertain and ambivalent and thereby lose many opportunities to advance the giving and generosity of the congregation. When you are confident of your mission, you become confident in asking for money.

The central purpose of this book is to help you discover the ways you can strengthen your own giving and the giving of your congregation. As you grow the mission, you will grow the giving. And as you grow the giving, you will be in a stronger position to focus your best energies on the mission.

The following four steps for giving are each covered in depth in later sections of this book.

1. *Grow the principles for giving.* There are seven principles for giving—and for living as well—namely, living is giving, people give to a winning cause, people have a spirit of generosity, people live forward toward positive expectancies, who asks who is decisive, people give to people, and have fun and live in Christ.

2. *Develop the possibilities for giving.* Six sources of giving are available to you and your congregation, namely, spontaneous giving, major community worship giving, special planned giving, short-term giving, annual giving, and enduring giving.

3. *Advance the motivations for giving.* These five motivations—compassion, community, challenge, reasonability, and commitment—plus positive reinforcement, are important.

4. *Build your understanding of stewardship.* God calls us to be good stewards in a most decisive time.

These four steps for giving are really also steps for mission. Study them and implement them. Individuals and congregations who practice these steps can advance their funding for outreach and mission. In turn, they will become strong, vital mission congregations, sharing their leadership and resources richly and fully in evangelism and mission.

Giving is living. These steps for giving are also steps for living. They will help you gain strength of purpose in your life and will assist you in your interactions with your family, your friends, the people you work with, and those you come into contact with in day-to-day life.

By implementing these four steps, individuals and congregations can advance their own generosity and the generosity of the group. The following chapters share practical suggestions and wisdom for applying these steps. As you follow these steps, you will grow the giving for the mission.

The following study possibilities can aid in your exploration of the four steps of giving:

- Lead a congregational study in the fall, winter, or spring.
- Invite your adult classes and other adult groupings to study this book.
- Focus on one of the steps in your board meetings and/or other key leader group meetings.
- Share in a Mission and Giving Discovery Retreat, which can help people discover their longings toward mission and giving.
- Invite your finance committee to study this book.
- Lead a study group of campaign workers and key leaders prior to a giving campaign.

You will discover many other study possibilities. Tell people in your congregation that studying this book will be helpful to them in their mission, their life, their family, and their church.

After studying these steps, develop an action plan for implementing them. Take into account how they can best be applied in your own life and in your congregation. Keep the following guidelines in mind when developing your plan:

- Competencies
- Value in the community
- Having fun
- Promise for your future mission
- God's calling for you

In which of the four steps do your best competencies and strengths lie? Build on these strengths to grow forward. By doing better what you do best, you will be in the strongest position to tackle your weaknessess.

If you begin with your weaknesses, you will be in the weakest position to tackle them.

Evaluate which of these four steps you are already doing reasonably well. Then advance and improve them so they are strong and excellent.

In what ways can these four steps for giving have added value in your community? A congregation teaches its members certain attitudes and behavior patterns about giving. A congregation also teaches groups in the community certain values about money. You can help community groups learn constructive attitudes, values, and behavior patterns concerning giving.

Which of the four steps would you have fun advancing first? Select first the steps that you would genuinely enjoy working on as a leader, pastor, or congregation.

Which steps have promise for the future mission of your congregation? Look ahead to the coming years. Advance first those steps that will strengthen your life and give momentum to your congregation. In this way you will advance the promise of your future mission.

Select the two giving steps you can implement now. Improve on your "best shots." Grow and develop them. Then focus on the remaining steps. By using this developmental strategy, you will significantly advance your own life and giving. You will help your congregation realize its promise and grow in generosity in its mission and its giving.

In what ways is God's calling inviting you to grow your living and your giving? In what ways is God's calling leading your congregation forward in mission and giving?

God's calling comes to us in many ways. Sometimes the calling comes to us in those areas we do best. Sometimes we hear the calling through our anxieties and anticipations. Sometimes we discover God's calling through other people. Sometimes God's calling comes to us directly. As you study the four steps for giving, listen for God's calling in your life.

The first step is to grow the principles for giving. These are principles for living life to its fullest. These principles help with both living and giving.

Chapter 2

A Winning Cause

People give to a winning cause, not to a sinking ship. This is the second principle for giving. The mission of God is a winning cause. Your congregation, at its best, is a winning cause.

- We are the Christmas people.
- We are the Easter people.
- We are the people of the Open Tomb.
- We are the people of the Risen Lord.

God calls us to the winning cause of mission. People will be helped. Lives will be changed. There will be times of reconciliation, wholeness, caring, and justice. Much will be accomplished through mission.

Beyond times of defeat, despair, depression, and despondency, there is Easter. In the midst of dark valleys and deep shadows, there is faith, hope, love, giving. Overcoming sin and tragedy, there is the resurrection. The mission of God endures. The love of God endures. Discover the ways in which God is helping you and your congregation to be a people of faith, to be a mission people, to be an Easter people, to be a winning cause. Rejoice in these and give thanks.

When you describe your church as a sinking ship, you will reach fewer people and raise less money. To be sure, you will raise a little money—just enough money to delude yourself that the sinking-ship approach works. When you focus on God's mission, you will reach more people; you will raise the money for the mission. God's mission is a winning cause, not a sinking ship.

Congregations with the spirit of a winning cause have key leaders, grassroots, and a pastoral team whose best gifts are:

- growing,

- developing,

- advancing,

- building.

We have a variety of gifts. Some have gifts in planning, or teaching, or shepherding, or music, or evangelism. Some have the gift of growing, of developing, of advancing, of building.

Whenever faith, hope, and love are present richly and fully in a congregation, you will find people with the gifts of growing, developing, advancing, and building. Select those having these gifts as your leaders. Grow these gifts in yourself.

Congregations that convey the spirit of a sinking ship usually have some dominant persons among the leadership whose "best gifts" are:

- complaining,

- lamenting,

- scolding,

- whining.

I encourage you to not select those for leadership who are predisposed to displaying these questionable "gifts." Try to avoid growing these "gifts" in yourself. They produce negative results.

Complainers raise doubt. Lamenters generate a spirit of doom and gloom. Lamenting that "things are not going well in our church's finances" creates a climate of despair, not an atmosphere of generosity and giving. Scolders inspire anger. Whiners create pity. Such negative people spend each meeting studying the finance figures and "sitting on their pity pot." Their pattern is pity. They whine, "If people were only more committed, our finances would be better."

In quiet, relentless ways, they seem to almost enjoy scolding the congregation and whining over the current plight. They may do so politely and gently, hardly ever raising their voices, but the damage is done nonetheless. They often use the language of commitment to scold the congregation. They almost relish saying, "People are not living up to the commitments they made when they took their membership vows."

Somewhere they learned these patterns of behavior. Maybe they learned from scolding parents. Maybe they learned from other authority figures who scolded and scared them. Whatever the source of their behavior, you can count on and depend on this: the more scolding is done in your congregation, the more anger will be raised. The more whining is done, the more unhealthy pity will be generated. Generosity and giving will be diminished, not increased, by such negative approaches.

People lead in direct relation to the way they experience being led. When they hear complaining, lamenting, scolding, and whining in their church, they will simply learn that complaining, lamenting, scolding, and whining are acceptable behavior patterns in their personal lives. The art in life—and in giving—is to help people experience the positive behavior patterns of growing, developing, advancing, and building.

Again and again, people parallel the behavior of their leaders. In many congregations, the leaders and the pastor have a confident, assured spirit. They do not waver and falter even when they occasionally experience defeat and disappointment. They are aware of their own mistakes and of their own deeper sins, and yet they live with a confidence in themselves and the grassroots of the congregation. Their lives reflect the strength of their confidence in the mission of God.

In other congregations there is a spirit of failure and remorse. The leaders and the pastor have no confidence, or at best only a tenuous confidence in the grassroots of their congregation. There is a pervasive sense of defeat and a cloud of gloom.

The leadership model you provide will help determine how others around you will pattern their leadership. The leaders in your congregation will lead as you lead them.

Whenever the leadership team adopts a stance of complaining, lamenting, scolding, and whining, other leaders and grassroots members will adopt that same stance. Whenever the leadership team is

- growing,
- developing,
- advancing,
- and building,

this will create leaders and grassroots members that grow, develop, advance, and build.

Discover persons whose best gifts are in growing, developing, advancing, and building. They live life with the spirit of a winning cause. Grow these gifts in yourself.

Persons with the gift of growing help others to flourish and become their best true selves. They nurture their own growth and the growth of those around them. They encourage confidence and assurance in individuals and groups.

Those with the gift of developing discern new possibilities and opportunities. They discover ways to move forward. They see fresh options that assist individuals and groups to move toward innovative possibilities.

Persons with the gift of advancing share compassion and encouragement in ways that help others to progress in their life's pilgrimage. They share by coaching, not correcting. They help individuals and groups discover their best motivational resources for living and giving.

Those with the gift of building nurture vision and hope. They focus on the whole, not the parts—on the long view, not the limited view. They help set realistic and achievable goals. They assist individuals and groups to unite toward mission.

Persons with these qualities and gifts advance your faith and the faith of your congregation. Recruit for your leadership team those who have these gifts. With the encouragement of such a team, people will give generously and graciously.

Consider your own life. Do you live with the confidence that you are part of a winning cause? Do your own best gifts include growing and developing, advancing and building?

Consider how you relate to your family, those you work with, and those you meet in everyday ordinary life. Is your primary impulse to share the gifts of growing, developing, advancing, and building?

Do you spend more time growing your life or complaining about your plight? Do you invest more energy in developing your new possibilities and opportunities or in lamenting being stuck where you are?

Do you spend more time compassionately advancing and encouraging persons or scolding them? Do you build and nurture people with your vision and hope, or do you whine about this or that? Check where, more often than not, you think you are on Table 2.1.

	Present and Frequent	Somewhat Present	Somewhat Present	Solid and Strong
complaining lamenting scolding whining				growing developing advancing building
Yourself				
Key Leaders				
Grassroots				
Pastoral Team				

Table 2.1

Place the following prayer on your refrigerator, your desk, in your wallet or purse, in your car, or on the bathroom mirror. Pray this prayer each day of your life. Live this prayer with your family and friends, with those you work with, and with those you are in mission with. Help make this be the prayer of personal growth of your congregation.

With the help of God, my family and friends,

I am

growing confidence and assurance

in myself and others,

developing new possibilities and opportunities,

advancing compassion and encouragement,

and building vision and hope.

I pray I will complain and lament less.

I pray that I will forget how to scold and whine.

God help me to grow, develop, advance, and build.

Amen.

Discover the steps you can take to nurture these gifts, strengths and competencies even more fully in your own life, your family, and your congregation.

Next, consider the key leaders, the grassroots, and the pastoral team. In which way, more often than not, do the key leaders tend to relate to the grassroots of the congregation? What about the grassroots and the pastoral team? Check where you think each grouping is on Table 2.1.

The congration will reflect the spirit of a winning cause when you, your key leaders, the grassroots, and the pastoral team enhance and nurture the gifts of growing, developing, advancing, and building. Discover ways to grow these gifts even more richly and fully.

In some congregations, a few persons may have a peculiar "theology of the cross." Their focus, particularly when it comes to giving, is primarily on the crucifixion. Their premise seems to be that guilt should motivate giving. Their plea is, "Christ died for your sins; show your gratitude with your pledge." They are trying to grow the giving on guilt.

They seem to believe that the Christian message ends on the cross. But it does not end on the cross. It begins in fresh, new ways with the open tomb, the risen Lord, and new life in Christ. The disciples thought they had placed their hopes on a sinking ship when Christ's body was taken down from the cross and placed in the tomb. With the resurrection, they discovered anew that they were part of a winning cause.

The Gospel writers knew the end of the story. In fact, they saw the end as a new beginning. Because they knew of Christ's resurrection, they traced back from the resurrection to tell of the incarnation, life, and death of Christ. It is quite clear that the Christian community that gathered during that first century lived with an abiding confidence in a risen Lord. It is as a result of their acceptance of the risen Lord that we understand what took place on Golgotha.

Christ invites you to live as a risen person. Christ invites you to new life. Christ invites you to live life at its fullest and best and to give generously and graciously on behalf of God's mission.

Christ's death on the cross is an act of generosity and grace. Yes, it is an amazing sacrifice. And yes, in even larger and richer ways, Christ's death on the cross reveals the generosity and graciousness of God's love. This grace is even more fully advanced with our risen Lord.

I am encouraging you to have a theology of resurrection as well as a theology of the cross. I am suggesting that you invite people to their risen life in Christ. Don't let your giving campaigns focus only on what happened on Golgotha. Help them focus on the meaning of the open tomb, the risen Lord, the new life in Christ, and the winning cause of God's mission on this planet.

Be part of a winning cause. Help your congregation be part of a winning cause. Give your life to the mission of God.

People are drawn to a winning cause. People are not drawn to groups that complain, lament, scold, and whine. Most of them already have enough of these negatives in their lives. People are drawn to groups that help them to grow, develop, advance, and build their lives.

Those congregations having the confidence that they are participating in the winning cause of God's mission are the congregations that grow forward the generosity of their people. The more you describe your church as a winning cause, the more people you will reach and the more giving you will raise.

People give to a winning cause, not a sinking ship. Share—with honesty and integrity—the ways in which you and your congregation are participating in a winning cause. We are the resurrection people. We are the Easter people. We are the people of hope.

Chapter 3

A Spirit of Generosity

People have a genuine spirit of generosity. This is the third principle of giving. We have this spirit of generosity because of Whose we are, not who we are.

God's nature reflects amazing grace and generosity with us. When we live forward to our best true selves, we are living forward to the image and likeness in which God created us. When we do not live forward to our best true selves, we may behave in stingy and selfish ways. We may be greedy and grabby.

Sometimes we are self-centered in driving, desperate, futile ways. These behaviors are symptoms of our fear, which is evidence of our sense of separation from God's love. In this life's pilgrimage, we become fearful and afraid.

There is a direct correlation between our fears and our stingy behavior. The more frightened we feel in our life's pilgrimage, the more we wrestle with our fears. The more we wrestle with our fears, the more preoccupied we become with ourselves, and the more selfish we become. Our stingy and selfish behavior are our ways of trying to reassure ourselves amidst our own fear.

Likewise, emotionally scarred people behave in selfish ways. Sometimes, damaging, painful, tragic events scar and mar our lives. When we are scarred, we become greedy and grabby. As a mechanism of self-protection, we focus on ourselves. This self-centeredness is the only way we know—at this moment in our life's pilgrimage—to deal with the scars of life.

Sometimes, we are both scared and scarred. It does little good to lecture yourself or others about being stingy and selfish, greedy and grabby, because these are only symptoms.

Instead, focus on and seek to understand your fear. Sense the calming, restoring spirit of God. Know that even though we are scared and scarred, the healing grace and generosity of God is present with us. Be at peace. God is with us. God is love.

In our time of mission, it is crucial that we help persons discover enduring sources of hope. There are some who bemoan the materialism of our culture and the materialism of others in their congregation. They feel that too many people are preoccupied with the material things of this life. When people grab for the material symbols of success in greedy, selfish ways, it is a symptom of a deeper problem. In our time, there is a vacuum of hope. Materialism is only the symptom. The lack of hope is the real problem.

The primary reason people are drawn to the material, the "flimsies" of this life, is that they are looking for some fleeting sense of hope. They see no stable and reliable sources of hope in their present or in their immediate future, so they grasp at objects. They grab for a new car, a new boat, or new clothes, for this gadget or that gimmick, for a house or a vacation—they try to buy hope by purchasing the flimsies of this life.

For one instant, they may feel a momentary, transitory sense of hope, of reassurance, of stability. But then comes the first dent in the new car, the first scratch on the new boat. The gadget breaks. The gimmick is out of fashion. The fleeting sense of hope vanishes.

People live on hope, not on memory. Take away a person's memories and they become anxious. Take away a person's hopes and they become terrified. God's amazing grace and compassion help us find hope in the present and the immediate future.

God invites us to be the Easter people—the people who have a confident sense of hope and trust. God's presence is both now here and now there. The presence of God is found in every event of reconciliation, wholeness, caring, and justice. We live with the confidence of God's presence.

When we discover we are the Easter people, we begin to express God's presence in our lives; it becomes manifest in a loving spirit of generosity. People who have discovered and accepted the healing grace and compassion of God live in hope and generosity.

As we discover God's presence in our hearts and lives, we are able to share grace and generosity with others—our family and friends, business associates, people in the community and in our congregation.

God is compelling and persistent in bestowing grace and generosity, even when we willfully turn away from God. Amidst the deep tragedies that mar and scar our lives, amidst all those times we have been neglected and abused, amidst our own self-abuse and self-neglect, amidst our own stubbornness and sinfulness, God welcomes us back with the generous gift of forgiveness and grace.

We can grow beyond scaredness, scarredness, and sinfulness as we grow to know Whose we are. We find hope and generosity when we accept the grace and generous gifts of God.

People have a genuine spirit of generosity. We want our lives to count in enduring ways. Most of us hope we will have an impact in lasting ways as we raise our children and pass on to them a sense of grace and compassion, integrity and character, wisdom and judgment, hope and peace. In everyday, ordinary life, we hope our lives will have enduring value as we touch others' lives.

In our time, many people experience a pervasive sense of powerlessness. They feel the decisions that shape their lives and affect their destinies are made somewhere else, by someone else, and they can't quite figure out who, where, or why.

Apathy and anger are two symptoms of this pervasive sense of powerlessness. When a pastor tells me of the problem of apathy in a congregation, I know it is not simply connected with the church. The apathy in the church is only a symptom of a greater powerlessness people feel over their lives.

Sometimes this sense of powerlessness shows up as anger, causing someone to explode over a petty, picky little matter and making us wonder why the argument is taking place at all. The anger is not really connected to the issue; it is only a symptom of the feeling of powerlessness.

Some people feel a driving need to rediscover their personal power so that they can feel that their life's destiny is within their grasp. As people regain a sense of their own power, they are in a stronger position to share their confidence and generosity.

In interview after interview, people teach me that they want their lives to count in missional, relational ways more than in organizational, institutional ways. They teach me that they want to relate in meaningful ways with their family, with their friends, and with their community. They want to make a difference in constructive ways with the people in their congregation and with the people they seek to reach in the name of Christ. They want their lives to count in mission.

Even though we sometimes feel powerless, even though we are sometimes lazy and indifferent, troubled or wasteful of our lives, there is in us a persistent, deeply felt yearning and longing that our lives count in helpful, enduring ways. Just as we know the grave is before us, just as we live in the hope we will be with God in the next life, we also hope that we will leave something behind that shows our life made a difference.

There is a sense of stirring excitement—a sense of growth and development—as people find themselves participating in a mission team that generously offers concrete, effective help with specific human hurts and hopes.

People often "put up with" an institutional organization. They have a fleeting hope that somehow, amidst all those committee meetings, their lives will matter in a missional, relational way. People are not compellingly drawn to give money in order to save an institution or an organization. They are not moved to stop decline.

We want our lives to matter. We want some sense of power to choose ways that our lives can count. We want our lives to make a difference in missional, relational ways that advance the movement of God's mission on this planet.

It is easier to raise money in a mission environment in which people's lives count. It is harder to raise money in an organizational, institutional environment in which the primary focus is on saving monuments—buildings, equipment, maintenance.

People want their lives to count by growing a movement, not a monument. People are not drawn primarily to buildings, organizational matters, business needs. Rather, they want to do something specific and concrete that will help make their lives meaningful.

When a congregation has a mission-building committee, rather than a building-building committee, it will grow the mission. In growing the mission they may invest:

- one year in the design of their blueprint for their mission,

- one year in raising the additional funds to advance and grow their mission,

- and a third year in constructing their very specific, concrete missional outreach toward specific human hurts and hopes.

These congregations invest as much intentional leadership, creativity, and energy in growing the mission as they would in building a building. People will throng to generously help support a mission that is specific and concrete.

Think of those who have been generous with you. Picture, in your mind's eye, one or more persons who have an enduring spirit of generosity. You may recall a good friend or a member of your family. Think of the rich, full ways in which they share their laughter, their grace, their generosity.

These are not codependent people. Do not confuse generosity and codependency. A codependent shares more help than would be helpful. This overhelpfulness becomes harmful, creating a pattern of codependency. For whatever reasons, codependents want to have others dependent on them. They give not out of generosity but out of a need to manipulate a codependent relationship. That is not giving.

We live through this life's pilgrimage with the deep, compelling, abiding grace and generosity of God. No person is an island. We do not live this life's pilgrimage by ourselves, or even with only a few close friends. Although we do not always know, recognize, fully appreciate, and appropriate God's presence in our lives, God is always there for us.

Even when we have tried to be an island and closed ourselves off, it is God who builds a bridge from the mainland to our island. God builds a bridge so that we might discover in Whose image and likeness we are made.

In these times, many of us frequently experience a sense of loneliness and lostness. There is much alienation and compartmentalization, dehumanization and fragmentation in our lives. In our loneliness and lostness, God seeks us out. We are not alone. We are not lost. Even when we have carried ourselves into the far country, God is with us there.

In our wanderings, we may waste our inheritance. It is the very presence of God with us that helps us come to our senses—to awaken us to the mess we have made of our lives, the pigsty we have got ourselves into.

As we head home, it is God who sees us from a long way off. God runs to us with grace and compassion, forgiveness and generosity. It is God who says,

> "This child of mine was dead and has come to
> life again; was lost, and has been found."

Luke 15:24.

God's compassion is God's way of helping us know Whose we are. When people discover Whose they are, they grow a genuine spirit of generosity.

Chapter 4

Expectancies

People live forward or downward to our expectancies with them. This is the fourth principle of giving. Our expectancies shape the perceptions persons have of themselves. Perception yields behavior; behavior yields destiny. In one ancient text, the following verse can be found:

- Sow a thought, reap an action.

- Sow an action, reap a habit.

- Sow a habit, reap a character.

- Sow a character, reap a destiny.

Our perceptions shape the ways we behave. The ways we behave shape our destiny.

A football team with the perception that it is a losing team behaves and acts like a losing team. Given enough time, the team creates for itself the destiny of a losing season. The choir with the perception that it does not sing very well sings in a faltering, off-key way. The student who perceives him- or herself a poor student becomes a poor student. Given enough time, and all those with negative perceptions of themselves reap the destiny they expect.

How can this destructive cycle be changed? A wise, caring teacher comes along with a newfound expectancy and helps them to a newfound perception. Based on that newfound perception, there is a newfound behavior. From this newfound behavior, there is a newfound destiny.

Think of the mentor, the teacher, the family member, the friend who has meant much to you in the growing of your own life. Many of us are who we are today because some wise, caring person helped us to grow forward to their expectancies with us. They helped us discover a new perception, behavior, and destiny.

Many of us are who we are today because Christ has come into our lives with the expectancy of His grace. Christ helps us to a newfound perception, behavior, and destiny. Out of that newfound perception, we behave in newfound ways. We live forward to the expectancies of our Lord.

Here is an important point: People live forward to positively communicated expectancies, but people live downward to negatively communicated expectations. The word *expectation* has about it a character of legalism and law—hard-nosed, picky and petty, top down. It is as though expectations are mandated and obligatory. We back away from rigid expectations. However, the word *expectancies* has an anticipatory and encouraging quality. Expectancies promote an open-ended pilgrimage, a growing and developing spirit. Expectancies have more to do with grace and compassion than with legalism and law. People live forward to our expectancies with them. People live forward to grace and compassion.

I met Sam when he was twenty-three years of age. As he was growing up, his mother would look at his school report cards and say,

Sammy, you can do better.

Even when he earned excellent reports, she would say, "Sammy, you can do better." The words had the ring of expectations.

When he was elected president of the high school, he heard her say, "Sammy, you can do better." At the university, he made excellent grades, was starting quarterback on the varsity football team and a leader in the student government. Her comment continued to be, "Sammy, you can do better."

As a young man he was selected for special honors—"Sammy, you can do better." Always he would hear, "Sammy, you can do better."

His translation was:

Sammy, you never succeed. You always fail.

His mother meant well. She thought her words were a way of sharing encouragement. This supposed encouragement from his mother caused Sam to develop a poor self-image, to believe that he always failed, that he never quite lived up to the expectancies of his mother. Indeed, her expectancies had turned into expectations.

At twenty-three years of age, Sam had developed an identity of failure—that is, whenever he got close to success, he would marshal all his strengths and competencies to ensure that he would fail yet another time. He was in the process of making a mess of his life.

Sam could never remember a time when someone appreciatively said,

Well done.

With the grace of God, Sam was able to discover constructive expectancies and to live forward to them. In time he developed the confidence that he could say to himself, "Well done." He could hear the words of others who said to him, "Well done." He could know that God was saying to him, "Well done, thou good and faithful servant."

The perceptions we have of ourselves shape our behavior. The expectancies others have of us also shape our behavior. The two go hand in hand. We learn some of our self-perceptions from others' expectancies of us.

We not only respond to the expectancies of others around us, we also continue to respond to the expectancies of those who are no longer with us, whose expectancies we still carry with us in memory.

In many congregations year after year someone will have said to the congregation,

You can do better.

Repeated year after year, this statement reinforces the congregation's perception that it has not lived forward to the expectancies of the leaders and the pastor. Again, the expectancies turn into expectations and reinforce the feeling of never quite fulfilling those expectations. That identity of failure nurtures the low self-esteem pervasive in too many congregations. As a result, congregations year after year live downward to the expectations their leaders have of them.

Once during a giving campaign in our congregation, we had gathered at one member's office where we could use a number of telephone lines. Over the course of the evening, I could hear the person in the next office as he phoned members of our congregation. When someone answered, he would say,

Hello. My name is Jim Johnson from Pleasant Valley Church. We're having our fund-raising campaign. I don't suppose you'd be willing to make a pledge, would you?

He was the only worker that night who achieved 100 percent consistency. Every person he contacted lived downward to his expectancies of them. Everyone said no.

In contrast, I heard many others say,

> Hello. I'm Mary Smith with Pleasant Valley congregation. We're in the midst of our giving campaign. We would appreciate very much your giving generously to the mission of the church during the coming year.

To this constructive invitation, many would respond,

> Yes. Sure. I'll give. Put me down for $_____ amount.

Whether you invite persons to give during a personal visit, by telephone, or in a small group gathering, follow these guidelines. You will help these people live forward to their best generosity.

- Share simply and gently who you are.

- Share who you are with, not where you are at or from. *With* is mutual and relational; *at* and *from* are distancing, location words. "I am Bill Jones with Pleasant Valley congregation" is more personal than "I am Bill Jones from (or at) Pleasant Valley Church."

- Share appreciation on the front end of the invitation.

- Give people a chance to give generously.

- Focus on the mission of the congregation, not on the budget.

- Share a spirit of "Thank you" and positively reinforce the generosity of their giving.

The word *only* is deadly. In some congregations during a campaign, someone will stand up and announce,

> We have received pledges totalling only
> $92,000 toward our goal of $100,000.

The word *only* is a word worth giving up for Lent. *Only* teaches the congregation that they have not done well. It belittles and devalues what has been achieved and accomplished. It creates a perception that we have a long way to go. It's like the coach saying to the team,

> You have scored only 92,000 points. You're still
> behind. I'm not sure you are going to win.

You can more constructively say,

> This is a generous congregation. Already people have
> contributed pledges totalling $92,000 toward our goal of
> $100,000. Thank you. We will very much appreciate, count
> on, and depend on your help in raising the remaining
> $8,000.

This approach is more like the coach who shares appreciation for the 92,000 points that have been scored and then invites the team to their best effort toward achieving the remaining 8,000 points.

A team that plays to win performs differently from a team that plays to avoid losing. For example, in a national championship basketball game, one team that had a fast break and a full court press was more than twenty points ahead by half time. This team played an intense, energized, fast-moving, rapid-breaking approach to the game. In the third quarter, they lost their lead and fell miserably behind. The announcer asked the co-announcer (a former well-known, successful coach) what had happened. The co-announcer said,

> I've always taught my teams "we play to win." In the
> first half that's what this team did. After half time they
> changed. They began to play to avoid losing, and they got
> off their game.

In the first half, the team lived forward to their expectancies. In the second half, they lived downward to their expectations.

So it is with all of us—as individuals and as congregations. I have worked with many congregations across the years. Some congregations live with confidence and conviction,

> We play to win.

Some congregations seem to have the motto, "We play to avoid losing." There are a few congregations who seem to have the goal, "We play to lose." These congregations have developed an identity of failure. And then there are those few congregations who act like, "We are not sure we want to leave the locker room." Each of these negative expectancies contributes to the decline and death of congregations.

Each of us can make one of the following choices in our own lives and in our congregations:

- We play to win.

- We play to avoid losing.

- We play to lose.

- We are not sure we want to leave the locker room.

In something as fleeting as a basketball game, a team can decide, "We play to win." Similarly, in something as enduring as the mission of God, you and your congregation can decide, "We play to win."

Decide which of these four directions is the way forward for your own life. Decide which is the way forward for you and your congregation. For you it comes down to, finally, a philosophy of life. For your congregation it comes down to a theology of the Christian mission.

Grow your own life. Develop creative expectancies for yourself. Grow positive expectancies with your congregation. People share their lives and their giving generously as they live forward to constructive expectancies.

Chapter 5

The Decisive Factor

Who asks who is decisive. The person doing the asking is the most decisive factor in giving. This is the fifth principle of giving. How the invitation is shared also plays a determining role. It is often how you share the invitation that inspires another person to generous giving. The stronger the match between you and the person you are asking, the more likely the individual will be to give generously and graciously to the mission of your congregation.

The act of asking is in itself decisive. When someone says, "Will you marry me?" the simple act of asking begins the covenant. Without the asking, the marriage does not happen. Similarly, someone might ask, "Have you discovered Christ in your life?" and with the asking, so begins the journey.

In giving campaigns, there is an old saying,

> The contribution not yet given is
> the contribution not yet asked for.

It is always amazing to discover how willing people are to give when they are graciously asked. The spirit of the asking is decisive. Gracious asking results in generous giving. Half-hearted asking results in half-hearted giving. The best way to ask is in the spirit of compassion and with a sense of community.

The invitation to giving may be shared in a variety of ways. Sometimes the invitation is shared personally—in person or by phone. Sometimes the invitation to giving is shared in informal small group gatherings. Sometimes it is offered in large congregational gatherings or in worship services.

Sometimes the invitation to giving is shared in a personal note, a letter, or a series of letters. Sometimes the invitation is shared through brochures that describe the mission, telling who will be helped and who will be doing the helping.

Any of these—and many more—are ways in which the invitation to giving can be shared. Whatever the method of invitation, who asks who to give is decisive.

In our time, people live in five "neighborhoods" each of which significantly influences their life's pilgrimage. These five neighborhoods are:

- relational

- vocational

- sociological

- geographical

- genealogical.

The predominant, primary neighborhood affecting people's lives is their relational neighborhood. This neighborhood consists of the informal and formal relationships of sharing and caring friends and acquaintances—an "adopted" extended family that enriches and supports a person's life. To be sure, one's family of origin is also frequently part of this relational neighborhood.

This relational neighborhood network develops informal, sustaining, everyday, ordinary life

- goals and values

- customs, habits, and traditions

- communication and language system

- leadership and decision-making processes

- sacred places of meeting

- common, shared visions of the future.

In our time, the family is often primarily developed in this relational neighborhood network wherein people help one another every day—in life's celebrative events and in life's moments of dark tragedy. People create and develop their own relational neighborhoods as they live day by day.

Closely related to the relational neighborhood is the vocational neighborhood. This neighborhood is also instrumental in developing goals, values, customs, habits, traditions, and so on.

Given the high percentage of families in which both spouses work outside the home, and given the time, energy, and effort we invest in our vocations, those with whom we work become an important vocational village that informs and enriches our lives. Sometimes this vocational neighborhood so closely overlaps the relational neighborhood that it is hard to separate the two.

People also live in a sociological neighborhood, which, like the other neighborhoods, helps develop goals, values, customs, habits, traditions, and so on. In these sociological groupings, we share common economic and cultural influences. Our sociological neighborhood influences the ways in which we live out our lives in our relational and vocational neighborhoods. Frequently, these three neighborhoods overlap in important ways.

People also live in a geographical neighborhood. Years ago, many people in a congregation shared much the same relational, vocational, sociological, and geographical neighborhoods. Because of this, churches once were able to organize their members into geographical neighborhood groups. These "neighborhood groups" worked because of relational, and to a lesser extent vocational and sociological, reasons and not primarily for geographical reasons.

In certain neighborhoods there still exists an overlaying of relational, vocational, and sociological neighborhoods, and in such neighborhoods it would still work to organize giving efforts geographically. But today people rarely live primarily in a geographical neighborhood. The increased mobility of people makes it possible for them to create a relational neighborhood and to form an informal extended family far across the community.

Individuals live their whole lives with the imprinting of the genealogical, or biological, neighborhood into which they were born. It is less common that people's genealogical neighborhood significantly overlays the relational neighborhood networks in which they live out their lives.

There is currently a breakdown of many genealogical extended family clans and a subsequent loss of many genealogically based families. These developments have led many to look for a sense of family within a significant relational neighborhood. In many cases the genealogical neighborhood may not be able to deliver the sense of roots, place, belonging, the sense of sharing and caring, the sense of family and friends that used to help support people in their foundational life search for community.

It is important to understand that all five of these neighborhoods—to a greater or lesser degree—are operative in each person's life pilgrimage. And it is important to understand that geographical proximity is often the least effective criterion for deciding who asks who.

It works better when you organize your giving campaigns along relational neighborhoods. It is more helpful to have people in your congregation call on someone in their relational, vocational, or sociological neighborhood. Individuals who are called on by someone who lives in the same geographical neighborhood may not respond as generously as they would respond to someone in their relational neighborhood.

Leaders of successful giving campaigns identify a number of significant relational groupings within the congregation. Each of these groups will have a different "best person" who can share the invitation to give with their significant relational grouping.

Some congregations already have an intuitive understanding of this foundational principle, which is evident in how callers select those they will call upon. The art is to help those in your giving campaign develop a fuller understanding of the five neighborhoods in which people live. Once your people understand these five neighborhoods, invite them to:

> Feel free to select people who are in their relational, vocational, or sociological neighborhoods. If a person selected also happens to live in the same geographical neighborhood, that is an added plus.

The purpose of a giving campaign is to help persons grow their giving. It confuses and blurs the focus to ask callers to have two purposes: (1) to invite people they contact to advance forward their giving and, in addition, (2) to contact someone who lives in their geographical neighborhood for the purpose of "getting to know each other better."

It is fine to create many other occasions of fellowship in which people who live in the same geographical neighborhood and also happen to be members of the same congregation can gather together. But keep this goal separate from your giving campaign.

The primary focus should be on helping people advance the generosity of their giving. The art is to have a good match of who asks who for the money, so that both will be on the same motivational wavelength, have a common shared vision of the future, and help to grow forward each other's generosity in giving. People share their giving generously when the invitation comes from someone decisive in their life.

Chapter 6

People

People give to people. This is the sixth giving principle. People do not give to budget details and campaign goals.

It is a fallacy to think that the more carefully each line item of a budget is explained, the more people will give. This type of thinking is based on the premise that the more information people have, the more they will be motivated to give.

However, this usually is the case only for those who have strong analytical competencies. Extensive line-item explanations create analysis paralysis. People feel overwhelmed by getting more information than they had questions.

Most importantly, education is not the same as motivation. People often believe that campaign thermometer goals—usually shown in red—motivate people to give. And these goals do motivate some people to give—but usually only those who have had a hand in developing the budget.

Achieving budget goals is not a primary motivator for the grassroots of a congregation. The grassroots does not have ultimate ownership for whether the budget is met. But the grassroots does have considerable ownership for whether people are helped.

To be sure, budget details and thermometer goals can be somewhat helpful in fund-raising efforts. But it is unwise to rely primarily on these as a way to invite people to give.

People give to people, not to brochures and mailings. Some giving campaigns seem to be based on the premise that the more mailings sent out, the more money will be raised.

Certainly, repetition is an important factor in giving campaigns. If a story is shared in several ways, people are more likely to respond. At the same time, too many brochures and too many mailings end up creating resistance and resentment. And when people feel hassled, they become hesitant to give; their generosity is squelched.

The other extreme is not providing enough information. Some churches take pride in sending out only one letter and brochure to raise funds to meet the budget. Each year they support a conservative budget with a modest percentage increase. This is the way they've done it for years.

One wonders how much money these congregations would be generously capable of giving were the principles for giving put more fully into practice. One wonders at all the money that wasn't raised that could have been—money that has been lost and will never go toward God's mission.

A creative, people-centered, mission-focused brochure that communicates compassion and community is very effective. Invitational letters—positive and constructive—are also helpful but should not be excessive.

Keep in mind that people give money to people, not to brochures and mailings and not to pretties and programs. To a certain extent, we all are drawn to the most recent "pretty"—the latest gimmick, the most recent fad, the current fashion. In our desire for quick closure, immediate satisfaction, short-term results, we sometimes hope the latest pretty will do the trick. And it may, for the moment. But this approach is not lasting. In the long term it has a limited, marginal return.

Some people imagine that a focus on programs will help, and it does—some. Emphasizing programs is perhaps the most constructive giving approach mentioned thus far. Yet the drawback is that this approach frequently comes across as institutional and functional. The focus is usually too much on the programs in and of themselves and not enough on the people served in and through those programs and activities. People give money to people, not to functional, institutional programs.

Why do so many churches focus on budget details and thermometer goals, brochures and mailings, pretties and programs as a means to promote giving? Over years of considering this question I have seen that there are two primary underlying causes.

First, the people who plan the budget are the ones who have ownership for the budget. They want the congregation to have ownership for it as well. Often many of the same people who plan the budget are also involved in raising the money to meet the budget. Hence, the focus of their giving campaign is on what they have ownership for, namely, money to meet the budget.

Second, a budget is often compiled by people with highly analytical competencies. Their detailed explanations of the budget line items are based on the assumption that information generates giving—and among those with similar analytical skills, it does. But the vast majority of persons within the congregation, including those with strong analytical competencies, are primarily motivated by compassion and community, not by detailed analysis. It is a mistake to assume that what motivates budget planners will motivate the grassroots.

When people give, they have in mind, perhaps intuitively, three groupings of people. They give generously and graciously to:

- the people who are being helped

- the people who are helping

- the people who are leaders—those whose wisdom and vision share the invitation for giving.

People give to the people who will be helped. A little child gets stuck in a well, and people give resources to help in the rescue. A devastating hurricane, tornado, or earthquake strikes, and people generously send their support to help those in trouble. In times of deep need, sudden tragedy, and great catastrophe, people give generously—to help other people.

In quieter, less desperate times, people give steadfastly and solidly to help people. They give to help the youth in the congregation and the community. They give to help preschool families with their growth and development. They give to help the elderly. They give to help the poor. They give to help persons with specific human hurts and hopes. They give to help those who are grieving, recovering, or struggling to put their lives more fully together. People give to people as a way to share God's love with other people in their community, state, and across the planet.

People also give to the people who are helping. To be sure, when they give, people first have in mind the people who are being helped. But in addition, when people give, they think of the people who are helping.

For example, consider the Salvation Army. Again and again, when I ask people what comes to their mind when they hear the words *Salvation Army,* their first image is the poor, the people who are being helped. Equally strong is their second picture, which is the Salvation Army officer, the person who is doing the helping.

In your giving campaigns, tell about the youth who are being helped—and also tell about the youth counselors and the youth teachers who are sharing the help. People will give to help youth; they will also give to help the helping team.

Tell about the preschool families who are being helped, and also tell about the preschool teachers and resource leaders. People will give to help preschool families, and they will also give to support those who help.

Similarly, although it is important to focus on the elderly who are being helped, it is also important to give your congregation a picture of the leaders and resource people who help the elderly in your community. It is important to create the mental image of the people who are doing the helping.

Ultimately, the best helping is mutual and inclusive, not top-down and exclusive. Christ was asked the question,

Who is my neighbor?

Luke 10:29

In response, Christ shared the parable of the man who had been attacked by robbers and was left at the side of the road. One of the most compelling pictures over the centuries of the Christian movement has been that of the Good Samaritan, the unlikely person who stopped and helped the stricken man.

Who is the good neighbor? One thoughtful interpretation of the parable is that the good neighbor is the man who was attacked and left in the ditch. That is, the good neighbor is the one who brings forth the best in another person. The stricken man brought out the best in the Samaritan, the unlikeliest of the passersby, who over the centuries has come to be called the Good Samaritan.

Considered in this way, it is not always precisely clear who is helping whom. In a genuine sense, the people with whom we are in mission are helping us live our own lives at our best.

And finally, people give to the people who are leaders. In their mind's eye, people see those who are being helped, they see the helping team, and they see the leaders of the congregation. These leaders are those whose wisdom and vision have guided the congregational decisions for a specific mission budget. These leaders are those who share the invitation to give.

When the invitation to give occurs, the grassroots of the congregation see the picture of the leaders of the congregation. They see those who are serving as chair of the board, committee chairpersons, the pastor, and the staff. A constellation of leaders comes to mind, is quietly present.

When the grassroots of the congregation have confidence in the direction their leaders are leading, they respond generously with their giving. A successful giving campaign illustrates the confidence of the grassroots in the leaders of the congregation.

The important point is that people give generously and graciously to these groups: the people who will be helped, the people who are helping, and the people who are leading the mission. People give to people.

Thus, describe your mission budget by creating pictures of who will be helped. Share several compelling pictures. Also include several images of those who are helping. And share the names or a picture of all the leaders who participated in creating the congregation's mission budget.

Someone might ask, "Shouldn't people give money to God?" meaning that if we describe our giving campaign as "giving to God," won't that help us raise more money?

The answer is yes—with this important qualification. For those who have lived many years in the Christian life, the invitation to "give money to God" will have considerable resonance and power. When you seek to advance giving among a group of longtime Christians, a focus on "giving back to God" is helpful.

However, there are many in the congregation who are relatively new to the faith. Hopefully, you are reaching many persons new to the Christian life, and for them, such an invitation will not yet be meaningful in the same way.

Remember that in the parable, the priest passed by on the other side of the road; he was tending to religious matters. Likewise, the Levite passed by on the other side of the road. It was only the Samaritan, the most unlikely of the three, who stopped to help the person in need. Jesus said,

> "Which of these three do you think proved to be a neighbor to the man who fell into the robbers' hands?"
>
> And he [the lawyer] said, "The one who showed mercy toward him."
>
> And Jesus said to him, "Go and do the same."
>
> *Luke 10:36–37*

The neighbor is the one who shows mercy. Just so, God invites us to show mercy and compassion in our giving. Do not ask the question "Shouldn't people give money to God?" Ask instead the wiser question "To whom does God want us to give?"

Jesus said,

> "For I was hungry, and you gave me something to eat; I was thirsty, and you gave Me drink; I was a stranger, and you invited Me in; naked, and you clothed Me; I was sick, and you visited Me; I was in prison, and you came to Me."
>
> Then the righteous will answer Him, saying ". . . When did we do these things . . . ?"
>
> "Truly I say to you, to the extent that you did it to one of these brothers of Mine, even the least of them, you did it to Me."
>
> *Matt. 25:35–40*

In that last great accounting, the focus will be on our compassion with our neighbors. Christ's invitation is that we care for our brothers and sisters, that we give to people.

People are willing to share their giving generously with others. People are not motivated to give to budget details and thermometer goals, brochures and mailings, pretties and programs.

Grow the giving of your congregation. Grow the giving principle that people give to people.

Chapter 7

Living in Christ

Relax, have fun, enjoy life, live in Christ. This is the seventh principle of giving. Live your life in the presence of Christ. Surround yourself with the grace and peace of Christ.

In some congregations, people try really hard to raise money. They worry and fret. They become tense and anxious. They are determined not to fail. They seem to feel that if they don't reach their giving goal, many calamities will befall their congregation.

This pattern of worry, fretfulness, tension, and anxiety is handed down from one leadership team to the next. The finance committee and the board become the resident custodians of the anxiety legend.

This behavior pattern increases during giving campaigns. Yet despite all the worry and anxiety, the campaign succeeds in raising only a little money.

Regrettably, just enough money is raised to allow them to think that the behavior pattern works. The little money raised reinforces the anxious, fretful behavior, and so the pattern is repeated year after year. Compared to the energy expended in worry, the amount of new money raised is disproportionately low.

In sports, a team that is tense and tight does not play well. Baseball players who go to the plate anxious and fretful, determined to hit a home run on every swing of the bat, do one thing very well: they strike out. When they dig in, clench their teeth, tighten their muscles, determined to hit a home run on every pitch, their batting average is dismal.

The art is to go to the plate with a relaxed intentionality. Hit a single. Bunt down the first-base line. Hit a blazing grounder to the shortstop, who then bobbles the ball. Beat the throw to first. Hit another grounder. Strike out. Hit a single. Strike out again. Earn a walk. Try to bunt down the third-base line. The player who has a specific objective that is reasonable and achievable and who has a relaxed intentionality will have a strong batting average.

Be at peace. You are more likely to raise more money when you are at peace. Some campaign leaders and fund-raisers imagine that in order to raise money it is necessary to get worked up into a frenzy of worry. "If we do not raise this budget, desperate calamities will befall us." By haranguing the team, they imagine the team will do better work. People who are tense and tight do not do a good job of asking for money. They press and push, prod and pressure others. They focus on commitment and want quick closure.

People who are relaxed do a better job of asking for money. The decisive moment in any giving campaign is the moment of asking, the moment of invitation. When the person being asked senses relaxed confidence and genuine intentionality behind the invitation, he or she will give generously and graciously.

People are drawn to groups that are having good fun and good times. In the biblical sense, people are drawn to the wedding feast, to the great banquet. People are drawn to the Easter people.

Grassroots members and unchurched people long for and look for some semblance of community, roots, place, belonging. They look for a group that has discovered that, beyond the cross, there is an open tomb, the risen Lord, and new life in Christ.

Some campaign leaders, fund-raisers, and pastors communicate that a dreadful result will occur if the year's campaign is not successful. They seem to think that the best way to stimulate and motivate their workers and givers is to create a negative picture. People are neither drawn to nor motivated by doom and gloom. Unchurched people already have enough doom and gloom in their lives. They are not drawn to organizations that live out, focus on, and anticipate an impending apocalypse. This is also true for the grassroots of a congregation. When campaign leaders, fund-raisers, and pastors cry, "Wolf! Wolf!" there is a diminishing return among the grassroots.

In one congregation I worked with, the giving campaign focused on compassion and community; we were having fun. At the half-way point in the campaign, the outside fund-raiser—a highly respected consultant we had employed—prepared a chart to show the results to date. Based on these results, his chart also projected that we would fall woefully short of our goal.

His statistical research and previous pledge campaign experiences indicated that if the first half of the households had pledged $500,000, the remaining half would barely pledge $100,000. It had always worked out that way.

Now, at the halfway point in our campaign, five hundred households had pledged $500,000. They had actually done better than ever before and better than the fund-raiser had predicted. Many of them had increased their giving significantly.

Although we were only half way into the campaign, this fund-raiser wanted to show the workers these charts and projections. He wanted to make a big speech to impress on them the grave trouble we were in. He wanted them to bear down harder to avoid "losing" the campaign.

The campaign chairperson and I discussed the matter in the light of our chosen priorities of compassion, community, and having fun. We decided the charts would not be mentioned and the fund-raiser would not speak.

In a relaxed, good fun, good times manner, the campaign chairperson told the gathered workers that the first 500 households had done so much better than we had ever imagined they would. This was statistically true.

He went on to say that this had become the most joyous, good fun, good times giving campaign he had ever participated in. He encouraged the workers to go on and have fun in contacting the remaining 500 households. And they did. At the end of the campaign, the second 500 households had contributed $350,000—significantly more than the fund-raiser had projected.

I am convinced that if we had allowed doom and gloom into the campaign at the half-way point, the fund-raiser would have been right: the remaining 500 households would have only pledged $100,000. His prediction would have become a self-fulfilling prophecy.

People are their most generous best at a wedding feast, at a great banquet, at Christmas and Easter. Help that spirit of having fun be part of your campaigns. People will give generously and graciously.

Discover deep satisfaction in your life. Life is precious and short. The art of living is to live each moment with a sense of fullness and contentment, appreciation and anticipation. Genuinely enjoy, in the deepest sense, your life's pilgrimage. We sometimes spend and waste life as though we had a million years to live.

We are often so busy that we sometimes go through day after day hardly seeing the loved ones around us, hardly sensing the mission to which God calls us. We move from this worry to that fret, from this tenseness to that anxiety, from this concern to that need. It is as though we think our busy-ness will help us save our life.

Look to those moments in which God is richly and fully present. To be sure, God is present in our lives in every moment. Look especially to those moments when you fully sense the peace and compassion of the presence of God. Look to those moments when you sense the warm love of family and friends. God invites us to enjoy life at its deepest levels of satisfaction, contentment, peace, and appreciation.

People who are genuinely enjoying life do a better job of advancing their own giving and the giving of their congregation than people who are preoccupied with life's twists and turns or people who are busy with an endless merry-go-round of activities.

We are the Easter people. We are the people of the risen Lord. The Easter people are not the people who simply follow the trends of the times, as important as it is to understand these. The Easter people—the people who live in Christ, the people who live in prayer— are the people who shape the trends of the times, rather than simply following them. You are more likely to grow forward your giving and your congregation's giving as you live in Christ, develop your mission and raise your giving with genuine prayer.

Pray for the long haul, not for quick closure. Know well that this venture is not won or lost in a day, a month, or a year. Growing and developing the giving and generosity of your congregation does not usually happen overnight. Know that it does and will happen as you live in Christ and Christ lives in you.

People are not motivated to share their giving in an environment of worry and fretting, tenseness and anxiety. People share their giving generously as they relax, have fun, enjoy life, live in Christ.

Grow the giving principle—relax, have fun, enjoy life, live in Christ.

Principles for Giving

1. Decide which giving principles are already well in place in your life. Check these in the column "Well in Place."

2. Select the giving principles you can grow forward most easily in your life in year 1. Check in the column "Year 1."

3. Decide which giving principles can be developed best for years 2, 3, and 4. Check in the appropriate column.

	Well in Place	Year 1	Year 2	Year 3	Year 4
I will grow a life of mission and giving.					
I will give to a winning cause.					
I will practice a genuine spirit of generosity.					
I will live forward to my best expectancies.					
I will listen for God's calling in my life.					
I will give to people.					
I will relax, have fun, enjoy life, live in Christ.					

Each year positively reinforce the giving principles you have well in place. Be much in prayer. God will help you to grow forward the quality and soundness, strengths and mission of your life.

Principles for Giving

1. Decide which giving principles are already well in place in your congregation. Check these in the column "Well in Place."

2. Select the giving principles you can grow forward most easily in year 1. Check in the column "Year 1."

3. Decide which giving principles can be developed best for years 2, 3, and 4. Check in the appropriate column.

	Well in Place	Year 1	Year 2	Year 3	Year 4
Living is giving.					
People give to a winning cause.					
People have a genuine spirit of generosity.					
People live forward to our expectancies with them.					
Who asks who is decisive.					
People give money to people.					
Relax, have fun, enjoy life, live in Christ.					

Each year positively reinforce the giving principles you have well in place.

PART TWO

Possibilities for Giving

Chapter 8

Six Sources for Giving

I encourage you to develop the possibilities for giving. People give—generously and graciously, eagerly and cheerfully—to God's mission in six major ways. All of these sources for giving are available to you and your congregation.

I call these sources for giving the six "giving doors":

- spontaneous giving

- major community worship giving

- special planned giving

- short-term major project giving

- annual budget giving

- enduring giving

People move through distinctive stages in their giving pilgrimage as they learn to give generously. Most people do not move directly from dating to marriage overnight. Likewise, in the development of their giving, most people do not move directly from spontaneous giving to regular annual budget giving overnight.

God calls us to generous giving, cheerful giving, giving that flows abundantly and richly out of one's heart and soul. It is an art to help yourself and other people grow forward the spirit of generosity. By opening these six "giving doors," you can help both yourself and your congregation to do precisely that.

Spontaneous Giving. People give on impulse, not planning. People do many things on impulse. A spontaneous giving invitation occurs with little advance notification or preparation. There are no advance letters, phone calls, promotion, or education. The invitation is shared spontaneously and graciously. We give generously.

Someone on a Sunday morning, or in a large gathering of the congregation, might say,

> We have this chance to help. We invite you
> this morning to give generously to this cause.

When we fail to invite people to give generously and spontaneously, we ignore all the people who, at this moment in their giving development, are primarily at the spontaneous stage of giving. The money they would have given is lost.

Many churches will have opportunities for three to five spontaneous giving invitations during the course of a year. You may find it appropriate, in an unusual year, to participate in as many as six or seven spontaneous giving invitations.

A spontaneous giving invitation focuses on a worthwhile cause. It may be a major advance in mission that has newly emerged. It may be a sudden need or emergency—a family in a desperate plight, people in need due to a hurricane, flood, or famine. The important point is that it is a major, worthwhile need, not something like building a tool shed out behind the church.

The focus of the invitation is on generous giving. Do not ask for "whatever you can afford to give." That raises the question, "Can I afford to give anything?" and reduces the matter to what one is or is not able to afford. The focus on generous giving helps people to discover their own deeper resources in life and to know, "Sure, I can help. Sure, I'd be glad to give."

In a spontaneous giving invitation, it is decisive that the person inviting have strong confidence in the cause. This spirit of confidence is rooted in the qualities of conviction and compassion. The person is convinced that this is an important, urgent cause. And the person has the compassion—"the passion with"—that the congregation's generous giving will help greatly.

Major Community Worship Giving. A second way to increase your congregation's giving is to increase the number of participants (not the number of members). The more you advance the number of participants, the more the giving will grow forward.

Major community worship occasions are times in which a concentrated effort is made to invite to worship unchurched persons in the community. We would also invite to join us persons in the congregation who have not been regularly active as we gather in a worshipping congregation as many persons as possible to be in worship of God. Major community worship occasions provide a special opportunity for unchurched people to come to worship for the first time. These occasions are a way of "giving permission," helping unchurched people feel that they will not stand out.

We tend to take for granted the increased attendance on Christmas and Easter Sundays. Even in an unchurched culture on a rich mission field, Christmas and Easter can be major community worship occasions. I also encourage congregations to select six to eight other times during the year that can be major community worship occasions.

A major community worship service may center on:

- a life stage

- a specific human hurt and hope

- a community interest or concern

- a major mission grouping.

A major community worship service is not a "church" Sunday, as is, for instance, Pentecost. Have forty-two to forty-four church Sundays a year. Develop eight to ten major services, whether on Sunday, Saturday, or during the week, in which to share resources with the whole community.

For example, some congregations have a major community worship service specifically for those who are in their first year of retirement. Some congregations focus on families with small children. Still others share worship resources with those who have lost a loved one during the past year. Many rural congregations have a "homecoming Sunday," which is for the whole community as well as the church.

On Christmas and Easter we see participants we don't see often—inactive members, constituent families, and unchurched people in the community. These participants are teaching us that if they had a church home, it would be with us. Help these people feel welcome. Share with them other major community worship opportunities that encourage their participation in worship.

The progression of worship participation tends to follow this pattern: first, people worship on major community Sundays; then they worship occasionally; then, more frequently; and finally, regularly. As they advance their participation in worship of God, they also advance their giving.

A major community worship opportunity draws to the church on that Sunday morning people who are mid-range active members, barely active members, inactive members, constituent families, and unchurched people in the community. I encourage you to help your congregation have major community services eight to ten times a year, not just twice on Christmas and Easter.

To develop a major community worship opportunity, invite a small task force of individuals to provide leadership and have fun growing and developing those who will be invited. Here is an example of how it was done at one church:

> Three people each wrote personal notes to twenty families. These were mailed early in the week before a major community Sunday. As a result, sixty families received personal notes of invitation.
>
> Three other people developed a direct mail invitation to 300 other households of unchurched people living in the community. The sole focus was to invite them to that major community Sunday. The 300 households were selected to match with the focus of that Sunday.
>
> Ten other people phoned three different households each day, Monday through Friday, before the major community Sunday. Each of the ten contacted fifteen households. The team as a whole contacted 150 households with a personal phone invitation. These 150 households were distinct from those receiving personal or direct mail invitations.

For the work of three persons writing notes, three persons developing the mailing, and ten persons phoning, 510 households were contacted that week. On that major community Sunday, the congregation was amazed to find a larger worship attendance than on any previous Sunday in the history of that church, including Christmas and Easter.

Contact methods that work best in your community range widely from a personal note, to a mailing, to a personal phone call, to a personal visit. It is important to do the contacting during the week before the major community Sunday. Most people come to a major community Sunday on impulse, not planning.

Share a warm, welcoming invitation to participate in a specific major community Sunday. Don't say, "You should be there" or "You ought to be there." Help people know that the resources they will discover in worship will be helpful in their lives and destinies and that you look forward with eagerness to their being a part of the worshipping congregation for this special worship occasion.

Many congregations that have grown forward the generosity of the people in the congregation have eight to ten major community Sundays a year. There is clearly a direct correlation between participation and giving. The more frequently people participate, the more generously they give. It is not necessary to stress giving on a major community Sunday. Rather, the focus should be on helping people with their lives. By offering "handles" of help, home, and hope, we help others grow forward in the Christian life.

People who worship with us tend to give. As participation increases, giving increases. There is no direct correlation between membership and giving. I see any number of congregations in which the membership has increased but, for a variety of reasons, the participation level has plateaued. The giving has a tendency to plateau. People who are members, but who do not worship with us, tend not to give.

If you would like to grow the giving, increase the level of participation, not the number of members. The more you advance the level of participation, the more the giving will grow forward.

Special Planned Giving. In contrast to spontaneous giving, this third source for giving involves thoughtful advance planning. The focus of special planned giving is a special cause that has ongoing, long-term significance in God's mission. Frequently, the invitation will focus on an emerging mission priority the local congregation sees as important to its outreach in the community. Sometimes a special cause will be one that has had historic significance over the years for the congregation.

In preparing for special planned giving, a team of people might invest several months in developing education and information, motivation and inspiration. People are encouraged to plan ahead, to prayerfully and thoughtfully consider what God is calling them to give generously on this special occasion.

On a specific Sunday, the congregation is invited to give generously to this special planned offering. Sometimes, this special planned giving invitation is extended through Advent or Lent.

The focus of special planned giving usually has more to do with mission than mortar, more to do with people and groups and less to do with debt retirement or debt servicing.

Two to four special planned giving opportunities per year is adequate; more would be too many. It is important to develop a sense of balance in terms of the six giving doors.

Some congregations have created a policy of including the special giving causes in their unified budget. The result is that they close off this giving door. Those who would respond generously to the appeal for the special cause may not yet be at the stage of giving to the annual budget. Taking away this giving opportunity may mean that you will not receive any of their giving.

Short-Term Major Project Giving. Some possibilities for this fourth source for giving include:

- mission and outreach

- new program and future staffing

- new building

- capital improvements

- debt retirement or debt servicing

- a combination of two or three of the above.

Customarily, a short-term major project invites pledging gifts over a period of two to three years.

Sometimes I hear the lament,

> We have some persons who are contributing to the building
> fund who are not giving to our annual budget.

Note well: When you take away the opportunity to give to a short-term major project, you may not receive any of their giving. Don't lament. Give thanks.

People are in different stages in their pilgrimage of giving. Some people are drawn to contributing in major ways to a short-term project. Others happily contribute to the annual budget. There is a diversity of gifts, and there is a diversity of ways in which people share their generosity. Honor that diversity by making available all these sources of giving. Do not try to force people into a single mold.

Sometimes the proposal for a short-term major project giving comes from the finance committee or the trustees. Thus, their short-term projects frequently focus on a building fund to build new facilities, to pay off a building debt, or to finance capital improvements to older facilities.

Raising money for debt retirement is the hardest money to raise.

It is better to develop a creative mix of the possibilities for short-term major project giving. Put the focus on more than simply "paying down the debt." Give people the opportunity to contribute to a constructive combination of short-term major projects.

Short-term projects help those who are already giving generously to the annual budget go the second mile. Frequently, these people will generously do so. Short-term projects also help people who have recently begun their giving through spontaneous giving, major community worship, and special planned giving to advance their giving for a more extended period of time.

Sometimes, a short-term major project helps people who are already giving $20 a week to the annual budget to advance their giving for the short term by a quantum leap. They decide to contribute $10 a week for a three-year period to a short-term major project in the church. During those three years, they learn their way forward to giving a total of $30 a week. From their perspective, that is a 50 percent increase in their giving.

When you develop an imaginative and creative mission program for the annual budget the year following the conclusion of the three-year pledges, many people will continue their total level of giving. If they've been giving $20 to the annual budget and $10 to the short-term project just ended, they will likely say, "Yes, we can give $30 to the annual budget."

Thus, one value of short-term project giving is that it can also be the prelude to a quantum giving growth to the annual budget.

Annual Budget Giving. People give in direct relation to ways in which they receive their income. They cannot give any other way. The focus on regular giving to the budget is a comparatively recent phenomenon for local congregations. In earlier times in many farming communities, the focus was on generous seasonal giving at the time of harvest. The giving principle was, "Give as the Lord prospers."

> Every one shall give as they are able, according to the blessing of the Lord your God which God has given you.
>
> *Deut. 16:17*

Although many people receive their income in equal periodic amounts, many people receive income in varying amounts from month to month. People's giving to an annual budget will usually follow the pattern of how they receive their income.

Regrettably, the finance committees of some congregations are preoccupied with annual budget giving. Since it is their responsibility to develop the annual budget, their focus becomes centered solely on this source for giving.

To be sure, it is important to raise support for the annual budget in the local congregation. But a related and even more important task is to help people in the congregation grow forward the generosity of their giving.

A preoccupation with annual budget support has a tendency to close the other five giving doors:

- closed—spontaneous giving

- closed—major community worship giving

- closed—special planned giving

- closed—short-term, major project giving

- open—annual budget giving

- closed—enduring giving

This tends to leave open only the giving door to support the annual budget, resulting in severe, regrettable consequences. The committee focuses solely on the annual budget because they want to know what is predictably going to come in. They close the other giving doors out of the mistaken notion that they compete with the support of the annual budget.

When a congregation focuses only on annual budget giving, they reap the following consequences:

- Only one of the six giving doors is made available to the people in that congregation.

- People's opportunities to grow forward their giving are severely limited.

- Such congregations receive only a portion of the total money that would have been given to their mission.

When a congregation develops a thoughtful plan that makes available all six sources of giving they enjoy the following advantages:

- They take seriously the distinctive ways through which people "come to discover" the generosity of their giving.

- People can take advantage of all six opportunities to grow forward their best giving.

- The congregation receives all the money people will generously and graciously contribute to God's mission.

A preoccupation with raising support for the annual budget limits your giving and the giving of your congregation. God calls us to generous giving, cheerful giving, giving that flows abundantly and richly out of one's heart and soul. The text does not say, "God loves a regular giver." What the text says is,

> Let each one do just as he has purposed in his heart; not grudgingly or under compulsion; for God loves a cheerful giver.
>
> *2 Cor. 9:7*

The art is to help people grow forward the generosity, the cheerfulness, of their giving.

Enduring Giving. People want their lives to count in enduring ways. From time to time, people look for ways to give enduring gifts that will have lasting value in God's mission.

I encourage churches to identify five to eight enduring projects that have balance, integrity, and broad-based appeal. These projects should have something for mission and something for mortar, something for others and something for us, as well as sufficiently compelling interest so that people across the congregation are drawn to one or more of the enduring gift projects.

Encourage memorial gifts to be designated to one of these enduring projects. Without these five to eight major enduring gift projects, churches end up with fifty to seventy memorial accounts having $100 here, $400 there.

People give enduring gifts both while they are alive and also in their wills. If you focus your enduring giving only on having people remember the church in their wills, you will receive less than half the enduring gifts you would otherwise have received. Many people give enduring gifts generously and graciously during their lifetimes. In my companion book, *Effective Church Finances*, you will discover fuller resources to help you with enduring gifts.

I invite you to look at giving through the eyes of the giver, not through the eyes of those who are focused on support for only the annual budget. The giver gives in all six ways. Whenever a congregation's vision is narrowly focused on only one or two of these six sources for giving, there will be a substantive reduction in the total giving that would otherwise have been contributed toward God's mission.

These six sources for giving do not compete with each other. They are distinctive forms of giving. The more successful you are with one form of giving, the more successful you can be with the other forms. Success breeds success.

The congregations who do this best have a sense of pace and planning in terms of how these sources of giving are shared. A team of people can successfully figure out the best giving development plan for drawing on all six sources for giving. Let there be a rhythm and momentum in the invitations to the congregation to give generously to God's mission.

Share all six giving doors with a thoughtful, constructive plan that has the qualities of pace and invitation. When a congregation does this best, they do not excessively overdo any or all these sources for giving. The spirit is one of progress and growth, not excessiveness and insistence, not legalism and law. They share these six sources for giving with a sense of balance, integrity, and broad-based appeal. They also recognize that people are at distinctive stages in their pilgrimage of generosity and giving.

To be sure, there may have been a time when the special requests for giving became excessive. There may have been occasions where there were too many requests, pleas, and fund-raising projects. The solution is not to go from too many to too few. The solution is to develop a thoughtful, constructive plan of giving development.

Each of these giving doors can be wisely and constructively opened in your congregation when giving is approached with a sense of rhythm, balance, and planning. Such constructive planning will allow you to offer a wide range of people the opportunity to "come on board" where they are best able to do so in growing forward the generosity of their giving.

People share their giving generously when all six sources for giving are available. People are not motivated to share their generosity when only a few giving doors are open. Develop all of the giving possibilities with your congregation. Share them with a sense of solid balance, confident integrity, and a broad-based invitation.

Sources for Giving

With prayer, develop your personal growth plan for your own giving. Consider well the sources for giving that will help you grow forward your own best generosity.

1. Decide which sources for giving are already well in place in your own life. Check these in the column "Well in Place."

2. Select the sources for giving that you can grow forward most easily in your own life in year 1. Check in the column "Year 1."

3. Decide which sources for giving can be developed best in your own life for years 2, 3, and 4. Check in the appropriate column.

	Well in Place	Year 1	Year 2	Year 3	Year 4
Spontaneous giving					
Major community worship					
Special planned giving					
Short-term major projects					
Annual giving					
Enduring giving					

Each year positively reinforce the sources for giving you have well in place. Be much in prayer that God will help you to grow forward the spirit of your generosity.

Sources for Giving

With the help of God's grace, develop your congregation action plan for its own giving. Consider well the sources for giving that will help your congregation grow forward its own best generosity.

1. Decide which sources for giving are already well in place in your congregation. Check these in the column "Well in Place."

2. Select the sources for giving you can grow forward most easily in year 1. Check in the column "Year 1."

3. Decide which sources for giving can be developed best for years 2, 3, and 4. Check in the appropriate column.

	Well in Place	Year 1	Year 2	Year 3	Year 4
Spontaneous giving					
Major community worship					
Special planned giving					
Short-term major projects					
Annual giving					
Enduring giving					

Each year positively reinforce the sources for giving you have well in place. Be much in prayer that God will help your congregation to grow forward the spirit of your generosity.

PART THREE

Motivations for Giving

Chapter 9

Major Motivational Resources

It is important to advance the motivations for giving in yourself and your congregation. The five major motivational resources are:

- compassion
- community
- challenge
- reasonability
- commitment

These major motivational resources, plus positive reinforcement, will:

- reach people in mission,
- help them to become workers and leaders,
- help them to contribute generously of their money.

Although there may be others, these are the five major motivational resources that are present in all of us as a solid part of our personhood.

These are motivational *resources*. Motivation is basically internal, not external. Manipulation is external. These are the major, internal resources out of which people internally motivate themselves to become part of the congregation, to become workers and leaders, and to give generously.

Two of the major motivational resources are generally predominant at any given point in a person's life pilgrimage. No one is "locked into" the same two resources forever. Life is a search. Life is growth and development. You can intentionally grow and develop to predominance whichever two motivational resources you choose.

It is the same for a local church. All five major motivational resources are present among the key leaders, and two are generally predominant. Similarly, all five resources are present among the grassroots, and two are generally predominant. All five are present in the pastor and the staff, and two are generally predominant. All five are present with the unchurched of the community, and two are generally predominant.

The problem comes when the two predominant resources of the key leaders do not match the two that are predominant among the grassroots of the congregation. In many congregations the key leaders have motivations different from those of the grassroots members. Further, it isn't always the same two with the key leaders and pastor, on the one hand, and the grassroots members and unchurched, on the other hand.

Compassion means sharing, caring, giving, loving, serving, supporting. Many people do what they do in this life's pilgrimage out of a sense of compassion. They do what they do because of their love for their children, their love for their family, their love of their country, their love of God's mission. They do what they do out of a genuine sense of compassion. The Bible shows us how many times Jesus had compassion.

Community is good fun, good times, fellowship, affiliation, belonging, a sense of family and home. Many people do what they do out of a search for community. The extended family clan used to provide a spirit of community. Many people are drawn to a church because they hope that they will discover within the congregation a spirit of community.

Challenge is accomplishment, attainment, achievement. Some people "rise to the bait" of the challenge. For them, life is one challenge after another. People who have a tendency to be high achievers frequently motivate themselves by a sense of challenge.

Reasonability is data, analysis, logic, and thinking that "it makes good sense." Some people motivate themselves at various stages of life's pilgrimage out of the motivation of common sense. For them, a course of action must be reasonable before they take it.

Commitment is dedication, faithfulness, duty, obligation, vows, loyalty. Some people motivate themselves out of a sense of dedication and loyalty. They do what they do because they have made deeply felt commitments.

A Motivational Match. Table 9.1 shows an effective motivational match. Congregations with this match have a strong track record of action, implementation, and momentum in their mission and their giving.

However, in some congregations, challenge and commitment are the two predominant motivational resources among a church's key leaders, which is typical for those who have been in the faith and leaders for a long time. The two resources predominant among the grassroots members are compassion and community. Among pastors, the motivations will vary greatly from one pastor to the next. Frequently they are "challenge" and "commitment." The two most often present among the unchurched are " compassion" and " community." This can be seen graphically in Table 9.2.

Motivations	Key Leaders	Grassroots	Pastor	Unchurched
Compassion	X	X	X	X
Community	X	X	X	X
Challenge				
Reasonability				
Commitment				

Table 9.1

Motivations	Key Leaders	Grassroots	Pastor	Unchurched
Compassion		X		X
Community		X		X
Challenge	X		X	
Reasonability				
Commitment	X		X	

Table 9.2

You are looking at a motivational gap, a divergence, between the predominant motivational resources of the key leaders and pastor, on the one hand, and the grassroots members and the unchurched, on the other hand.

It is frequently lamented that the same few people do everything in a local congregation. One of the major reasons for this is that there is a motivational gap between the key leaders and the grassroots members.

Consider an analogy of radio wavelength frequencies. The key leaders, motivated by challenge and commitment, broadcast signals—that is, communicate—on the motivational wavelength frequencies of challenge and commitment. The grassroots members have tuned their radio wavelength frequency receivers to the motivations of compassion and community. There is no resonance—no match—between motivations. It is a motivational gap. The reception comes through like so much static.

Frequently, key leaders and pastors reinforce one another's motivations of challenge and commitment. To be sure, this may be a motivational match between the key leaders and the pastor. In meeting after meeting, they reinforce one another using the motivational resources of challenge and commitment. They fail to see the motivational gap between themselves and the grassroots members. They fail to realize they will reach the grassroots primarily on the basis of a mutual compassion and community. They fail to realize that any hope of being in mission with the unchurched will clearly need to grow on the basis of compassion and community.

People grow and develop, and often their primary motivations change—sometimes consciously, sometimes unconsciously. Many congregations have realized they have a motivational gap and have found ways to grow forward to a motivational match. When they achieve a motivational match, they are stronger in their mission in the community.

I find the following two points consistently true:

1. Congregations that deliver nine out of the twelve central characteristics of effective churches are strong, effective congregations.

2. Congregations that develop a motivational match between:

   key leaders

   grassroots members

pastor and staff

unchurched

are strong, effective congregations.

The following example can be helpful in understanding the interaction of motivational resources and giving. A church I was working with needed to raise money for a new fellowship hall and church school space. During one of our planning sessions, I introduced the key leaders to the motivational resources.

I invited them to list the five major motivational resources on a sheet of paper and then check the two they felt were most predominant among their key leaders. Independently and individually, each checked challenge and commitment.

Then I asked them to do the same for the grassroots. Each checked compassion and community. And so I said to them,

> If you want to raise most of your money from among the key leaders, be sure to launch the building fund campaign with a "loyalty Sunday" appealing to commitment. Be sure to have commitment pledge cards.

> Display a challenge thermometer goal for the campaign. At the campaign's end, you will have reached the goal. You will have raised most of your money from among the key leaders. And you will be quietly distressed that, once again, you did not get much support from the grassroots members.

They said, "We will need the help of our grassroots in this project." This was my counsel to them:

> If you want to raise most of your money from among the grassroots, launch the campaign with the best good fun, good times community supper this congregation has ever seen. Let it be, in the biblical sense, a wedding feast. Let it be a great banquet. And do not, in the last ten minutes, undo everything you have spent the evening accomplishing. Do not have someone stand and challenge them to this awesome building fund goal, telling them that if only they would deepen their commitment, they might make the challenge goal.

Instead, let people leave knowing they have had one of the best experiences of community in their lives. Let it be the kind of legendary evening people look back on, years hence, and say, "That was truly community."

And when you print the brochure describing the new building, show pictures of the people—children, youth, and adults—who will be helped by the programs and activities that will take place for years to come in the new facilities. Show the blueprint for mission, the blueprint for compassion, the blueprint for program.

And if you also want to show the blueprint for the building, show that blueprint somewhere near the back of the brochure. Use the brochure primarily to illustrate how people's lives and destinies will be helped in compassionate, constructive ways for many years to come.

The key leaders of this congregation were intrigued by these suggestions. They understood well the major motivational resources as we discussed them that evening. They decided to focus on compassion and community.

They held one of the best community suppers there ever was. Their brochures described with compassion the ways people would be helped by the new building. The result was that they raised more money than they thought they would, and they raised it mainly from among the grassroots.

Later they asked me, "Why is it that these grassroots members do not contribute more to our annual budget?" In response, I showed them how the motivational resources had affected the results:

In the building fund campaign, their messages communicated compassion and community, which matched the motivational resources of the grassroots, who were motivated to give generously.

But with the annual budget campaign, they were still trying to raise the funds based on messages appealing to commitment and challenge. These did not match with the motivational resources of the grassroots members. There was a motivational gap.

We tend to assume that what motivates us will motivate other people. Frequently, key leaders spend enough time in meetings with one another that they reinforce among themselves the motivations of commitment and challenge. Then they make the fatal mistake of assuming that the grassroots and the unchurched will respond to messages appealing to commitment and challenge as well. But this seldom happens.

A Mission Field. In declining or dying congregations, it becomes very clear. The predominant motivations among the key leaders are commitment and challenge. The only people left in the congregation are those *committed* to the *challenge* of keeping the bloomin' doors open. Everybody else has gone somewhere else. The key leaders say to me, "What we need is people with more commitment."

I usually ask them to recall what drew them to their congregation in the early years. They talk of a compassionate, shepherding pastor. They talk of the sense of community and belonging—the home—they found in the congregation.

I gently suggest to them,

> What drew you to this congregation in a churched culture forty years ago was compassion and community. We now live in an unchurched culture. We cannot expect to draw the unchurched based on messages of commitment and challenge.

> That is not what drew you. Why would you expect those motivations to draw them?

I usually go on to suggest that what is really needed in the congregation is people with more compassion and community, not more commitment and challenge.

A denominational group I worked with experienced a long, steady decrease in congregational giving to the denominational support. Some of their leaders described to me what had been happening. As I listened, I discovered that the following pattern had prevailed each year:

> Step 1. Most of the delegates selected to go to the annual meeting were grassroots people. They were motivated, at heart, by compassion and community.

> Step 2. Just prior to the annual meeting, the denominational leaders received the financial projections for the coming year, which

showed an increase in expenses and a decrease in projected congregational giving to the denomination's support. The deficit was growing.

Step 3. At the annual meeting, the denominational leaders asked the delegates to return to their congregations and challenge them to deepen their commitment and accept the challenge of paying out in full all of their allotted denominational support during the coming year.

Step 4. The delegates dutifully went back and did what they had been asked to do. They reported to their congregation that things were getting worse, that they had to accept the challenge and deepen their commitment to do better to overcome the ever-growing deficit.

The first problem with this pattern is that the delegates' primary motivations are compassion and community—yet they are being asked to focus on challenge and commitment. This puts them "off their game"; it doesn't match with their own strongest motivational resources.

The second problem is that the new money needed to resolve the projected shortfall is to be found among the grassroots. But the grassroots do not respond generously to appeals to commitment and challenge because they are motivated by compassion and community.

Fortunately, after years of this downward spiral, we were able to put some "handles" on what could be done. We put in place new steps that focused richly and strongly on compassion and community. We laid to rest the preoccupation with the growing deficit.

The leaders realized that it had taken a long time to get into the fix, and it would take several years to grow beyond it. The leaders came to understand motivational resources well, and they did an excellent job of growing forward the giving based on compassion and community.

In a churched culture forty years ago, it was "the thing to do" to go to church. There were many long-time Christians. You could draw people to a church, help them become workers and leaders, and encourage them to contribute money based on the motivational resources of commitment and challenge. Those motivations worked well in the context of a churched culture.

Motivations	Key Leaders	Grassroots	Pastor	Unchurched
Compassion				
Community				
Challenge				
Reasonability				

Table 9.3

It is a clear fact that we no longer live in a churched culture; we live in a mission field. As motivators, challenge and commitment do not work as well on a mission field. When it is not the thing to do to go to church, messages of challenge and commitment fall on deaf ears.

On a mission field, compassion and community are more helpful than challenge, reasonability, and commitment. To be sure, the last three play an important role. But compassion and community are more useful on a mission field.

Compassion and community are early motivations in the faith, and commitment remains a major motivational resource. I recognize and value its usefulness. Without commitment, the chart could have looked like the one shown in Table 9.3.

Commitment is an important motivational resource, and it takes the longest to develop. It is the motivational resource that comes later in the Christian pilgrimage. When someone says to me, "What we need in this church is people with more commitment," I reply, "You have just taught me that you are a long-time Christian." It takes people many years to nurture the motivational resource of commitment.

A New Perspective. The general impression in many congregations is that a few people usually give most of the money. For example, for a congregation of 300 households, we expect that the first 150 households contacted in a giving campaign pledge a substantial amount and that the pledge results from the remaining 150 households will be significantly less. This pattern is repeated year after year. The question remains, "Why is it this way?"

Usually, giving campaigns are organized by key leaders and pastors, who tend to be long-time committed Christians. Thus, they organize a campaign that "broadcasts" its messages on the "radio wavelength frequencies" of:

- commitment

- challenge.

There is a high enough density of key leaders in the first 150 households that this message resonates well with them. There is a motivational match, and therefore the first 150 households generously and graciously contribute a substantial amount.

Then the key leaders remember the pattern of previous years: they didn't do as well with the remaining 150 households. And so they increase the "decibel volume" of the messages being broadcast on the radio wavelength frequencies of commitment and challenge. In most congregations this is done very politely, using personal intensity rather than raising one's voice.

If the volume was ten decibels of commitment for the first 150 households, they will turn it up to forty for the remaining households. The focus again and again is on "Be loyal to your church," and "Remember your membership vows."

But the 150 grassroots households have their "radio receivers" tuned to:

- compassion

- community

and the forty decibels of commitment comes through as so much static.

All the focus on commitment does is create passive-aggressive behavior, low-grade hostility, subliminal resentment, and eruptive forms of anger among the grassroots. And as a result, not much money is raised.

You will best grow the giving among the grassroots when your messages communicate a spirit of compassion and a sense of community. Most charitable giving is raised out of compassion and community.

Books on stewardship are usually written by long-time committed Christians. As a result, the authors often suggest that stewardship means commitment. But it is important to remember that for many people, stewardship is compassion or community or reasonability, not just commitment.

Many people grow their stewardship out of a sense of compassion. Many grow their stewardship because of who we are as God's community. Many other people find their way to stewardship because for them it makes reasonable sense. Stewardship is more than commitment, more than challenge; it is part of being a compassionate human being.

Likewise, most of the books on discipleship are written by long-time committed Christians, and so we read that discipleship is commitment. Again, discipleship is compassion. Discipleship is who we are as God's community. It is not possible to simply reduce discipleship only to commitment.

If you want to raise money, advance stewardship, and deepen discipleship among long-time Christians, then you can focus more on commitment and challenge. But when you want to advance the giving, grow the stewardship, and deepen the discipleship among the grassroots members and the unchurched, then be sure to focus on the motivations of compassion and community.

Reasonability is a major motivational resource in communities with a high proportion of those for whom analysis and research are important components of their life's work and pilgrimage. The area called Silicon Valley in California has a high density of engineers, scientists, and computer experts. In this kind of community, a congregation can grow forward by focusing on the motivations of compassion or community and reasonability.

A university community has a high proportion of people for whom research, data, and analysis are major priorities. To reach the professors, graduate students, and technical staff in university communities, you might focus on compassion or community and reasonability. To reach undergraduate students, you still do best focusing on the motivations of compassion and community.

Compassion and Sacrifice. Having discovered these motivational resources in a Twelve Keys Seminar or during a consultation, someone often will say to me,"When are we finally going to get around to commitment?"

In the course of the seminar, they have come to understand that compassion and community are early motivators. And yet they know that commitment is what motivates them and is why they are loyal to their church. They may believe that the situation in their congregation is becoming desperate. They feel that if we don't address commitment soon, there won't be much of their church left.

It is not that we "finally get around to" commitment. Grassroots members and unchurched people discover the Christian life through compassion and community. As we richly and fully share with them the spirit of compassion and the sense of community in our own spiritual growth and development, they will grow forward—at their own pace—to a deepening sense of commitment.

Developing commitment is not something we can do to them or for them. It is something they will grow and develop themselves. What re-assures them—what gives them a sense of certainty, confidence, and se-curity—is that they are surrounded by a congregation that shares compassion and community.

Some giving campaigns use the phrase, "Not equal giving, but equal sacrifice." This is a helpful phrase, and one reason key leaders are at-tracted to using it is because their own sense of sacrificial giving grows out of their long-time dedication. They see giving sacrificially as an expression of commitment—and it is.

Sacrificial giving is an expression of compassion and of community as well. The phrase could be,

> Not equal giving, but equal compassion,

Or it could be

> Not equal giving, but equal community.

People sacrifice out of compassion. Parents sacrifice out of compas-sion for their children. Soldiers in war sacrifice their own lives out of com-passion for their buddies. Our understanding of Jesus' sacrifice on the cross is that he did this out of his love and compassion for us, not out of his commitment to us.

Sacrifice is not solely commitment. More often than not, people sac-rifice out of a spirit of compassion and a sense of community.

It is amazing how often we innocently focus on the motivation of commitment when, in fact, it is not as helpful on a mission field. At the conclusion of the worship service, the last hymn could be the hymn of compassion, the hymn of community, the hymn of mission. It does not always have to be the hymn of dedication or the hymn of commitment. We could sometimes have a "love Sunday," not a "loyalty Sunday." We could have compassion cards or mission cards instead of commitment cards. Our newsletters, bulletins, notices, and announcements could use words that suggest compassion and community rather than commitment and challenge.

It is sometimes tough to share compassion. Occasionally, someone will say to me,

> Yes, we understand we may need to use the "easy ways" of compassion to reach grassroots in our church and the unchurched in our community. But isn't that a cheap gospel?

They say this on the assumption that compassion is easy and commitment is tough. Quite the opposite is true. It is difficult to live a life of compassion. It is even more difficult to share compassion.

Recall a time someone grievously harmed you or a time someone betrayed you. It takes all our resources of compassion to forgive these people. Reconciliation does not come easily. Whenever we give up our grudges; forgive the hurts; move beyond gossip, bitterness, and resentment; reconcile with someone from whom we have been alienated and estranged, it is tough to share compassion.

Compassion is often a hard choice in our life's pilgrimage. It is easier to ignore others and focus on self-love. It is easier to get caught up with the flimsies of this life. It is hard to love someone who disappoints you, to forgive someone who harms you, to have compassion for someone who hurts you.

Motivation and Mission. In many congregations, the existence of a motivational gap can eventually result in a loss of grassroots members and a decline in new people. The congregation will decline and, if no change occurs, may die.

As is represented visually in Table 9.4, whenever challenge and commitment or reasonability and commitment become the predominant motivational resources among key leaders and pastor, there will be a serious motivational gap between them and the grassroots and the unchurched.

It is helpful to build a motivational match as a means of moving beyond the problem of a motivational gap.

Motivations	Key Leaders	Grassroots	Pastor	Unchurched
Compassion		X		X
Community		X		X
Challenge	X		X	
Reasonability	(x)		(x)	
Commitment	X (x)		X (x)	

Table 9.4

I invite key leaders to create a motivational match from where they are to where the grassroots and the unchurched are. I encourage them to rediscover what drew them to the Christian life in their early years in the faith. I ask them to remember those who shared compassion with them and to recall the sense of community—of roots, place, belonging, good fun, good times, home, family—they found in their early congregation.

Then I often say to them:

> From today forward, I invite you to *accept the challenge* and *make the commitment* of doing whatever you do out of *compassion* and *community.*

You would be amazed at how many key leaders rise to this challenge and make the commitment. They rediscover the major motivational resources that drew them to the Christian life. They build a motivational bridge. And from that day forward, they accept the challenge and make the commitment to live with the motivational resources of compassion and community.

They create a motivational match between the key leaders, the grassroots, the pastor, and the unchurched, as can be seen in Table 9.5. This puts them in the strongest position to reach people in mission and help them become workers and leaders and to contribute generously of their giving.

Motivations	Key Leaders	Grassroots	Pastor	Unchurched
Compassion	↗X	X	↗X	X
Community	X ↴	X	X ↴	X
Challenge	○		○	
Reasonability				
Commitment	○		○	

Table 9.5

We learn as much by what the New Testament does not say as by what it does say. The text does not say, "For God was so committed to the world . . ." The text says,

For God so loved the world . . .

John 3:16

The text does not say, "We are committed to Jesus because Jesus was first committed to us." What the text does say is,

We love because He first loved us.

1 John 4:19

Again and again in the gospels, it is frequently said, "Jesus had compassion for the multitudes."

The two great commandments are:

You shall love the Lord your God with all your heart, and with all your soul, and with all your mind.

Matt. 22:37

and

You shall love your neighbor as yourself.

Matt. 22:39

The texts invite compassion and community as the primary motivational resources.

Most churches' membership vows were written by long-time dedicated Christians. Because of this, new members frequently are asked,

> Will you be loyal (commitment) to the
> denominational church and uphold it by your
> prayers, your presence, your gifts, and your support?

On a mission field, new-member vows will be more effective when they are oriented toward compassion and community:

> Will you love the Lord your God?
>
> Will you love your neighbor as yourself?
>
> Will you live well in this mission community?
>
> Will you share richly in God's mission this day
> and in the years to come?

At the end of the Gospel of John, Jesus does not ask Peter, "Are you committed to me?" The question to Peter is,

> Do you love me? [compassion]
>
> Tend my sheep. [community]
>
> *John 21:15–17*

You will grow your own generosity and the generosity of your congregation best as you grow the spirit of compassion and the sense of community in your life. These motivational resources, plus positive reinforcement, will advance both your living and your giving.

Chapter 10

Positive Reinforcement

Positive reinforcement raises more giving than negative reinforcement. Be a source of encouragement. The art of advancing your congregation's giving is to build goodwill. For each dollar you raise, create three dollars worth of goodwill. Ultimately, people will generously contribute those three dollars.

When you create three dollars of ill will for each dollar you raise, you will never see those three dollars—and eventually you will lose that one dollar.

It is important to say thank you. Say thank you in as many ways as possible, so that people know that you genuinely appreciate what they are giving to advance God's mission. It is quite simple: positive reinforcement raises more giving than negative reinforcement.

It is true that negative reinforcement raises a little money—just enough "little money" so that people who have a propensity toward negative reinforcement think that it works. Negative reinforcement works almost well enough to convince some people that it really accomplishes something. And it does. It raises a little money.

Positive reinforcement is constructive coaching. It encourages in affirming, creative ways. Positive reinforcement communicates a spirit of grace and compassion, not legalism and law.

Positive reinforcement affirms that life is a search. We are together in a common pilgrimage. We grow and learn, discover and develop, with and from one another. Positive reinforcement nurtures and encourages; it helps people discover ways forward. Positive reinforcement delivers handles for help and hope that are simple and realistic. It enables people to grow and develop.

By contrast, negative reinforcement is correcting. It tells people what they have "done wrong," what they "cannot do," and what they "should do." Those who have a tendency toward scolding and complaining often are drawn to negative reinforcement because it gives them a chance to take a "correcting" posture toward others. But in an environment of negative reinforcement, people give less generously.

Through an encouraging and coaching spirit, positive reinforcement helps people discover what they can do. People grow themselves forward, both in their personal lives and in their giving.

In an environment of positive reinforcement, people give more generously because the positive reinforcement confirms people's spirit of generosity and creativity. We are each created in the image and likeness of God. When people are at their best, they have a genuine sense of generosity.

Sometimes doubts, distractions, and depression erode our spirit and our generosity. Sometimes we become scared or scarred. We become preoccupied with ourselves. Positive reinforcement helps us remember who we are at our best.

There is a correlation between having a propensity toward negative reinforcement and having a longing to be in authority. People who hunger for influence frequently use negative reinforcement as an exercise in power. It temporarily puts them in a superior, "top-down" position.

But there is no lasting power derived from negative reinforcement. The momentary "power surge" experienced while delivering a message of negative reinforcement can be addictive, but it does not last.

Positive reinforcement, on the other hand, does have enduring value. People who live in an environment of positive reinforcement become less afraid of making mistakes. They "try their wings," develop a sense of their own creativity. An environment of positive reinforcement assures them that their creativity is appreciated.

Julie and I have spent some time sailing on lakes and oceans. In our first crossing to the Bahamas, we left Ft. Lauderdale early in the evening. In a sailboat it is important to make the crossing overnight. You want to arrive at Bimini early in the morning so that you can see and avoid the coral reefs as you navigate the poorly marked channel into the harbor.

As we approached the entrance to the channel, we saw a freighter anchored near the channel. We decided that if we stayed closer to the freighter, the water would be deeper. One never quite forgets the sound of the crunch of a sailboat's keel on a coral reef.

We learned later that the captain of the freighter had been sailing in the Bahamas for over twenty years. And yet earlier that week he had successfully run the freighter onto the reef. The closer we were to the freighter, the closer we were to the reef.

A rising tide and a local fisherman helped us, and we finally got our boat off the reef. Fortunately, no damage was done. The saying in the Bahamas is

> The skipper who says he has never run aground is the
> skipper whose boat has never left the dock.

In an environment of negative reinforcement, people seek to avoid mistakes. The best way to avoid mistakes is to do nothing.

In an environment of positive reinforcement, people try, experiment, discover. People aren't afraid to "leave the dock."

It is important, in your life and in your congregation, to share positive recognition even when mistakes occur. The more positive the reinforcement, the higher the level of creativity in you and in your congregation. In an environment in which they can discover their spirit of generosity and creativity, people will share their best giving.

Positive reinforcement shares active appreciation with people for their giving, which is one of the ways they contribute to God's mission. When people give, they touch the lives and destinies of many who are discovering a new life in Christ. By their giving, people strengthen the character and quality of life in their community and advance the cause of peace and justice in the world.

When you share positive reinforcement, you help people know that their lives count. You help them to know that you do not take for granted what they are doing. Your profound, sincere, active appreciation helps people know their giving is decisive.

In contrast, negative reinforcement delivers "passive recognition" for what people are not doing. People who express negative reinforcement convey the message:

> We have done our part. You have not yet done your part.
> When are you going to do what you should be doing?

Some giving campaigns are built on this premise, and their letters, announcements, brochures, and bulletins have this tone and spirit. This expression of negative reinforcement is a way some people focus on themselves, assuring themselves of their own self-righteousness, that they have done their part.

Sometimes we are not yet fully confident of God's grace. We lose sight of the assurance that it is through God's grace that we have been saved. We begin to feel the need to work out our own salvation. This uncertainty manifests as our self-righteousness. It is ironic. We strive so hard to achieve what God has already given us—the grace of salvation.

Active appreciation helps people pass on the knowledge that we have been given this grace. People who experience appreciation share appreciation. People reflect in their behavior how they are treated.

People who are the recipients of active appreciation for their giving turn around and express active appreciation for what other people are doing in the congregation. They take their active appreciation home with them. They share their active appreciation with their loved ones, their family, their coworkers, and their community.

People who are subjected to negative reinforcement develop resentments toward those delivering the negative reinforcement, toward the whole group, and toward themselves. In this last form of internalized self-resentment, the resenters come to resent the resenters.

One way these individuals cope with their own self-resentment is by overcompensating with self-righteousness. The two go hand in hand: self-resentment eventually results in self-righteousness.

People who experience appreciation share appreciation. One of the significant results of positive reinforcement is that it grows a sense of genuine, profound, sincere appreciation in the whole community. In an environment of active appreciation, people live more fully and give more generously.

Positive reinforcement is the way people share the richness of their compassion and love for one another. People who experience the profound, deep sharing of compassion develop the confidence to be in a strong growth and development pilgrimage in their own lives and destinies.

In many congregations the problem is not the passivity of the people. The problem is the negative reinforcement from the leaders. Help your congregation away from negative reinforcement.

Positive reinforcement genuinely appreciates and thanks people for what they are doing. Positive reinforcement does not say,

> Well, that's what you should have been doing all along.

Instead, positive reinforcement says,

> Well done, thou good and faithful servant. You have been faithful over a little. I will now give you the chance to be faithful over much. Enter into the joy of your Master.
>
> *Matt. 25:21,23*

People who experience positive reinforcement put themselves in a strong growth and development stance in their own lives. Whether in education, coaching, business, music, art, or civic and community work—whatever the sphere of life, those in a strong growth and development stance benefit from positive reinforcement. So will your congregation benefit from positive reinforcement, and as it does, it will live more fully and give more generously.

People give more generously in an environment of positive reinforcement because positive reinforcement helps people achieve proactive, constructive behavior. People who benefit from positive reinforcement can move beyond primarily reactive and sometimes destructive behavior. They develop an anticipatory, forward-moving, proactive stance toward life. Their own sense of self-worth and their behavior become increasingly constructive and affirmative.

By contrast, negative reinforcement encourages passive-aggressive behavior. Watch a team with a coach who delivers negative reinforcement, or a class with a teacher who delivers negative reinforcement, or a board meeting in which a pastor, finance chair, or key leader delivers negative reinforcement. Notice how quickly passive-aggressive behavior develops.

Negative reinforcement is frequently delivered in polite, quiet, distinguished ways. People hardly ever raise their voices. They rarely ever betray their latent, internal anger. They are polite and gracious, thoughtful and "considerate," quiet—and very deadly.

People who deliver positive reinforcement sometimes become excited, joyful, enthusiastic. They can get carried away shouting strong encouragement to the team. To be sure, people who deliver positive reinforcement can also do so with grace, dignity, decorum, and good manners.

Positive reinforcement encourages people to be proactively and constructively helpful. By contrast, negative reinforcement develops codependency relationships. The person who delivers negative reinforcement is frequently looking for a codependent/dependent interaction. Negative reinforcement is a way of saying:

> You could have done better. You have not done what you should have done. I am here to help you do better. I am here to serve as your codependent, to help you to do what you cannot in and of yourself do well enough.

People who deliver negative reinforcement often just want to be "helpful." However, they frequently deliver more help than would be helpful. The help becomes harmful and creates a pattern of dependency.

Whether it is in alcoholism, in family relations, or in giving, very frequently, the person communicating the negative reinforcement usually wants to create a dependency pattern. Through their negative reinforcement, they become a codependent with the dependent. They want the other person to depend on their negative reinforcement as the source of "help."

People who share positive reinforcement are looking for mutual relationships. They are looking for ways to participate together in proactive, constructive forms of behavior. Their message is:

> I look forward to our sharing, working, and living together in Christ.

> I look forward to ways we can contribute to the mission of God.

Positive reinforcement helps persons discover their best creativity, strengths, gifts, and competencies.

Positive reinforcement raises more giving any day than negative reinforcement every day. This is because positive reinforcement:

- confirms people's spirit of generosity and solid creativity,

- shares active appreciation for what people are doing,

- helps people toward strong growth and development in their lives,

- helps people achieve proactive, constructive behavior in mission.

Persons who practice positive reinforcement will see these results in their lives. Congregations who practice positive reinforcement will see these results in their congregation. In advancing the giving of your congregation, practice positive reinforcement, and you will see the effects spill over into people's lives, their families, their work, and their mission.

Chapter 11

===========

Advancing Positive Reinforcement

Here are three things you can do to implement and improve the practice of positive reinforcement.

1. Develop life practices of positive reinforcement.

2. Understand the sources of negative reinforcement.

3. Share a spirit of "thank you."

Your life will be richer. The mission of your congregation will be stronger. And the giving of your congregation will become even more generous.

God's love surrounds us. As a life practice, help yourself and your congregation recognize that God's love is surrounding and enfolding each and every one of us. The more you sense the love of God, the easier it becomes to practice positive reinforcement in your life.

Positive reinforcement persists in many congregations because the participants accept the forgiving presence of God's love. Grassroots, key leaders, and pastor—all have the profound sense that their lives are surrounded by the grace of God.

Thus, they live in love and encouragement. The spirit of love and the gift of encouragement pervades the group. They are amazed at the ways in which God's compassion has entered their lives. Their own profound, positive reinforcement is deeply grounded in the grace of God.

In other congregations the focus is on discouragement, despair, and depression. The "grapevine" in these congregations can be ugly, mean, vicious, gossipy. There will sometimes be people who "delight" in the failures and difficulties of others and seem to thrive on their mishaps and misfortunes. Dejection and discouragement are their daily companions. Such people may have "head knowledge" of God's love, but they apparently don't have "heart knowledge."

In the many congregations in which positive reinforcement thrives, it is expressed in people's love and encouragement with each other. There the grapevine focuses on who is growing and developing, what is being accomplished and achieved, who is searching and discovering. The grapevine reflects encouragement, enthusiasm, and excitement at what is happening in people's lives. These congregations know God's love is richly present, and they live in love and encouragement.

As a life practice, you can help yourself and your congregation deal constructively with sin. By dealing with sin confessionally and constructively, you will be freed to practice positive reinforcement in your life.

Positive reinforcement is not a naive, whistling-in-the-dark, foolish optimism. Positive reinforcement understands the poverty of the human condition and the awesome predicament of our separation from God.

Positive reinforcement invites us to confession. Most people know their sins pretty well. They do not need to be reminded in the picky, petty manner of negative reinforcement. They need a way to move forward positively. Negative reinforcement finds fault. Its self-righteous stance gets in the way of honest confession. Positive reinforcement offers a constructive way to move ahead.

Congregations with a strong, vigorous environment of positive reinforcement have a strong theology of love and grace. Congregations with an environment of negative reinforcement tend to have a shallow, superficial theology of blame. A theology of grace takes sin more seriously than a theology of blame.

A theology of grace reflects an understanding that the state of sin is so serious, so perilous, so grievous a predicament that only the grace of God can redeem us. A theology of grace is not "easy" grace but rather a grace that is rich, full, strong, vigorous.

Congregations that live with the compassion of God's love take sin very seriously; they know it is through the amazing love of God that we can come into the fullness of life. In these congregations, there is an almost awed sense of positive reinforcement for what God has done and continues to do in our lives.

Fulfilling your foundational life searches is a part of your life's pilgrimage. As a life practice, help yourself and your congregation to move toward fulfilling the foundational life searches in the light of the Gospel. Positive reinforcement thrives better when people are fulfilling their foundational life searches for

- individuality,

- community,

- meaning,

- hope.

Life is a search; life is a pilgrimage. People long for and look for some fulfillment in these foundational life searches.

Congregations living with negative reinforcement, unhappy and complaining, are so scared and/or scarred that they have become preoccupied with themselves. They have withdrawn into a fortress mentality. They have left their foundational life searches at the side of the road in this life's pilgrimage.

By contrast, whenever people are actively working on these foundational life searches, they will find ways of communicating positive reinforcement. These people have discovered their capacity and competencies for their own growth and development. With the help of God's grace, they grow and develop their strengths. They grow and develop their mission in their own and others' lives and destinies.

In these congregations the focus is on progress, not perfection. These people see themselves as in a strong stage of growth and development, as progressing toward fulfilling their foundational life searches.

Another critical key to advancing positive reinforcement is to live God's mission. As a life practice, help yourself and your congregation live fully the mission of God. The more you participate in the mission, the more you will practice positive reinforcement in your life. Many individuals and congregations have a spirit of positive reinforcement because of their conviction and confidence that they are sharing in God's mission.

On a mission field, we will have our rich, full share of depression, despair, and despondency. That comes with the territory. These difficulties can foster negative reinforcement. Some people have regrettably assumed that the way to overcome despair is to achieve what is defined by the world as "success." The antidote to despair is mission, not "success."

The answer to despair is to actively share in God's mission. Thus, I encourage you to live confidently and competently, helping people with their lives and destinies on behalf of God's mission. This will result in persistent, present, powerful positive reinforcement in your life. People with the confidence that they are sharing in God's mission are in a solid position to deal with whatever despair, depression, and despondency comes their way.

It is also important to understand negative reinforcement. Most people innately know the results of negative reinforcement. They have seen what it has done in their lives as they were growing up, and in their children's lives as they have sought to raise them. They have seen what it does in work, community activities, and their congregation. Yet even with all this awareness, negative reinforcement continues to pervade our lives.

Negative reinforcement is a learned behavior pattern. Somewhere along the line, we learned this pattern from someone—our parents, peers, friends, teachers. They may not have intended to teach it to us. They even may have been trying to overcome it themselves. Nevertheless, for whatever reasons, we learned it from them. Whether it was in our growing-up years, our coming-of-age years, or in our more mature years, we somewhere began to imitate this behavior.

This pattern of negative reinforcement persists because it is a way of venting anger. Sometimes a congregation's key leaders develop a latent anger that the grassroots members are not "doing what they should be doing." Rather than understanding the dynamic of their anger and asking God's forgiveness—rather than accepting God's grace in the midst of their anger—some leaders choose to vent their anger through low-key, negative reinforcement.

In congregations that share positive reinforcement, there exist people who have learned constructive ways of dealing with their anger. It is not that they suppress anger. They know that some anger is appropriate, an important resource against the injustices and indecencies of this world. They know that where there is life, there is anger. The also know that where there is life, there is reconciliation and love. In the midst of love and encouragement, these people have found ways of constructively using the resource of their own anger.

Negative reinforcement persists because it is the way some people cope with depression. I was once working with a congregation in which there was a very identifiable small group of complaining people. For many years, they had always complained about everything. They complained when the sanctuary was too hot. They complained when the sanctuary was too cold. For them, the temperature was never right.

They complained that the pastor never visited. When the pastor visited, they complained the pastor wasn't in the office. They complained about one thing one day and the opposite thing the next day. This small group of people had developed among themselves a pattern of complaining that had gone on for more than three decades.

I asked one of the wise, caring leaders of the congregation to tell me about the group, because she had been around this group for many years. She said to me, "Dr. Callahan, I've observed over the years that some people who complain a lot are unhappy within themselves." This is one of the reasons negative reinforcement persists: some people are unhappy within themselves.

I encourage you to share with these unhappy people the richness of compassion and love. It is appropriate to honor well, understand, value, and have a rich appreciation for those who are experiencing deep depression. One does not reject them or put them down. But neither does one placate and please them.

A component of compassion is understanding. These people's behavior pattern of negative reinforcement is the way in which they are attempting to "work out," albeit destructively, their own depression. Offering them hope can help.

Another reason negative reinforcement persists is because of intermittent "payoff." People with a behavior pattern of negative reinforcement may often enjoy other people's responses of passive-aggressive behavior, low-grade hostility, subliminal resentment, and eruptive forms of anger. They look for the attention these responses generate.

They don't realize they are repelling the very people they would like to attract and that they are losing their credibility in terms of their leadership in the group. They will continue to repeat this behavior until something happens to cause them to change. The intermittent satisfaction they get causes this behavior to persist.

Discover as many ways as you can to share a spirit of "thank you." In your own life, share appreciation richly and fully with your family, your coworkers, and people with whom you come into contact in daily life.

In your congregation, look for ways to thank people for what they are doing in their giving. Do so with integrity, confidence, and assurance. Whether your congregation focuses on giving or on pledging or on tithing, find ways to say thank you.

A thank-you letter, personal phone call, or personal visit can be a way to positively reinforce people—whatever their form of giving. This is one of the simple ways in which you can share positive reinforcement.

Send people a confirmation thank-you note immediately upon receiving their pledge. Don't wait. In some churches, the giving campaign occurs near the end of the fiscal year. The campaign leaders frequently become so busy with the campaign that no thank-you letter is sent. Indeed, often the only confirmation of their pledge people receive is when they receive their new monthly or quarterly statement after the first month or the first quarter of the new fiscal year. This is a poor way to say thank you.

You can grow forward the success of your giving campaign when you have one or two people send thank-you confirmations the day after each pledge is received. See that a thank-you note is sent that does two things:

- thanks people for their pledge

- confirms their pledge.

Make the thank-you note as personal as possible. You will be amazed at what happens on the community grapevine. The second half of the congregation will be encouraged as word spreads that the first half of the congregation has received acknowledgment and a genuine sense of personal appreciation, goodwill, and positive reinforcement.

Send a special thank-you letter to those individuals and families who have pledged to increase their giving. It will be different from the regular thank-you letter for those who have kept their pledges the same. This special confirmation letter could say something like,

> We very much appreciate your increased giving for the
> mission of the congregation during the coming year.

Then go on to confirm their pledge.

When you honor, thank, and appreciate their increased giving, people are more likely to consider increasing their giving again at some future time. When you take the increase for granted, it is likely that they will stay on a giving plateau longer.

Send a special thank-you letter to those who are making a pledge for the first time. Whether they have been members of your congregation for a number of years or have occasionally given recorded contributions or have joined within recent years—whatever the reason, this is their first pledge, and it deserves recognition, as follows:

> We very much appreciate your decision to pledge to the mission of the congregation. It is most helpful. Thank you.

People live in relational neighborhoods with others who may not yet have made a pledge. The special honoring of pledges is an important form of positive reinforcement that will pass along a good message on the community grapevine.

Thank new members who have joined your congregation this year for their pledges. When they begin giving, send them a thank-you note. Help new members know that their giving means much to the mission of the congregation. It is particularly important that these thank-you letters be sent as soon as possible after receiving the pledges.

Send thank-you statements of contribution. Look at your statements of contribution through the eyes of the giver, and think how much a comment of recognition would be appreciated.

However, be sure not to do what one church was doing. They were sending statements of contributions to those who had given nothing and saying "thank you" on those statements. This was their inverted legalistic way of trying to grow guilt so that these people would do something. This approach does not help. Share a positive word of appreciation for what people are giving; don't try to "guilt trip" them to get them to give.

Some statements of contributions look too much like accounting documents. This is because they were designed by someone who is looking at the matter through the eyes of the finance committee. In many churches I've suggested that the financial secretary send out statements to those who are current in their giving and write these two words on the statement:

> Thank you.

This practice will help.

In one church, the financial secretary asked me, "Dr. Callahan, do you really think that will help?" I said, "Well, try it. See what happens."

I was there a year later for a follow-up consultation. She said to me with amazement,

> Dr. Callahan, I began doing what you suggested, and do you know what happened? People began to write me back thank-you notes, thanking me for thanking them.

It had been years in that congregation since anyone had thanked people for giving.

Send a thank-you note to those who have recorded contributions. Even if your church does have pledging, there will be those who do not pledge but who do make recorded contributions. Each time they make a recorded contribution, send them a thank-you note. The more positively they experience their giving, the more likely they are to decide to become pledging households.

Share a thank-you note with those who make a special gift. Some churches are under the wrong impression that they should discourage special gifts because they want all the money to go to the annual operating budget. As we discussed in the chapter, "Six Sources for Giving," this is a misguided notion.

People will give to the operating budget on a regular basis and from time to time they will also share special gifts. Thank them. They will share with you more special gifts.

Have the spirit of "thank you" in your newsletters and bulletin. "Give up for Lent" every temptation to put announcements in the newsletter or bulletins that chide and scold. Find creative and constructive ways of sharing positive reinforcement. Effectively communicate this in your newsletters and bulletins. Help people have the sense that they are part of a winning team, not a sinking ship.

Send a letter of encouragement *prior to* low giving months. Give up the "summer slump letter." Some congregations have sent out the summer slump letter for so many years that it has become a tradition.

The summer slump letter has three paragraphs:

Paragraph 1: "The church has gotten a little bit behind on its bills."

Paragraph 2: "The utility bills were higher than we expected."

Paragraph 3: "Could you please send a little money to help us catch up?"

There are only three things wrong with the summer slump letter; other than that, it is a perfectly good letter. These are the three things that are wrong:

Paragraph 1: "The church has gotten a little bit behind in its bills" reminds people that they are a little bit behind in their own bills. Do you know anybody who's ahead?

Paragraph 2: "The utility bills are higher than we expected" has just reduced the winning cause of Christ to a utility bill.

Paragraph 3: "Could you please send a little money to help us catch up?" results in just that—they send you a little money.

People live forward or downward to our expectancies with them. If you ask for a little money, that's what you will get—a little money. Regrettably, churches receive just enough money to make them think the letter works.

Give up the summer slump letter. It describes your congregation as a sinking ship. It is counterproductive and does not help. Send your letter of encouragement *prior to* a low giving month. Act in a proactive way. And send an encouraging letter, not a lamenting letter. Choose words that match best with your congregation and community, and communicate this spirit:

Paragraph 1: "Our church is doing solid work."

Paragraph 2: "The lives and destinies of many people are being helped."

Paragraph 3: "Thank you for the generosity of your giving."

You don't even have to say "send more money." They will. People give money to a winning cause, not a sinking ship.

Share positive encouragement in your reports. At your monthly and quarterly meetings, whoever gives the report can help it to be a coaching one, not a correcting one. Help make the report affirm and encourage, not deliver despair and discouragement. Find solid ways to communicate positive reinforcement through your reports and your meetings.

Some congregations have too many finance committee meetings, which does more harm than good. This is particularly true in congregations in which the tendency of the finance committee meeting is to focus on negative reinforcement.

If your finance committee is meeting each month, one of the best things you can do is to meet once a quarter, or slightly more often then that. You will reduce the number of meetings that share negative reinforcement. You will successfully have set aside several possibilities of negative reinforcement. That will help.

Meet as often as makes sense to have constructive meetings. Avoid a routine of "we're always behind" meetings. Advance a pattern of proactive, creative finance planning. Most finance committees can achieve excellent work and focus on major priorities in five to seven solid meetings a year. When the committee meets too often, it gets caught up in "80 percenters" and negative reinforcement.

Send a year-end thank-you letter. At the end of the year, send a letter to thank people for their giving during the past year. This letter may also include the record they will need for tax purposes, but there is too much preoccupation with that record. We provide the record as a service. The primary service you can deliver is to thank them for their giving.

All twelve of these thank-you possibilities are helpful. Develop an action plan for the coming four years. Put some of these ideas into practice this year. By the end of the four years, have all the objectives you selected well in place. Discover other ways of sharing the spirit of "thank you."

Kind people share positive reinforcement. There is a strength to their kindness. They look wisely for what people do well. People who deliver negative reinforcement can be cruel when they think they are being kind. The statement, "You can do better" is a hurtful message. It deepens the person's compulsiveness toward perfectionism and creates low self-esteem and a sense of failure.

Although the kind person does recognize weaknesses and shortcomings, mistakes and sins, this person will look beyond these.

Strong people share positive reinforcement. People with a strong, vigorous compassion deliver positive reinforcement. People who are preoccupied with weaknesses and shortcomings—their own or those of others—deliver negative reinforcement. Strong people deliver positive reinforcement—strong in the sense that they count on themselves and on others to live life at its best. They are not hard on themselves; they are not picky and petty. They do not constantly say, "You can do better." They have solid expectancies for how their lives can count.

Soft people deliver negative reinforcement—soft in a sense that they count on people to live downward to the few feeble expectancies they have for them and for themselves. Do not let anyone tell you that negative reinforcement is the way forward.

Some people say to a pastor, "Pastor, during this giving campaign, you've got to tell these people what they need to hear." And after a sermon of negative reinforcement, these people come up to the pastor and say, "You really told them this time."

What people really need to hear is the strong, rich, full grace of God. What people really need to hear is love and encouragement. What people really need to hear is that they can fulfill their life searches in the grace of God and in the community of this church. What people really need to hear is that they can live lives of growth and development. What people really need to hear is that they can share in God's mission, that their lives can count.

This is what people really need to hear. These are the foundational principles of help, hope, and home that people long for and look for. When you want to "give them something" during a stewardship campaign, give them this positive message and they will do well.

Positive reinforcement raises more money any day than negative reinforcement does every day. Positive reinforcement raises a people of God. Negative reinforcement lowers a people into a preoccupation with their own despair, depression, and despondency.

Positive reinforcement constructively advances people's lives and the generosity of their giving.

Motivational Resources

Consider where each group is in your congregation. With prayer and wisdom, discover how you can best grow forward a motivational match.

Motivations	Key Leaders	Grassroots	Pastor	Unchurched
Compassion				
Community				
Challenge				
Reasonability				
Commitment				

PERSONAL GROWTH ACTION WORKSHEET

Positive Reinforcement

With prayer, develop your personal growth plan. Consider well the positive reinforcement practices to which God is calling you. Select those positive reinforcement practices that will help you grow forward.

1. Decide which positive reinforcement practices are already well in place in your own life. Check these in the column "Well in Place."

2. Select the positive reinforcement practices you can grow forward most easily in year 1. Check in the column "Year 1."

3. Decide which positive reinforcement practices you can develop best for years 2, 3, and 4. Check in the appropriate column.

	Well in Place	Year 1	Year 2	Year 3	Year 4
I confirm the spirit of generosity and solid creativity in the people around me.					
I share active appreciation for what persons are doing.					
I help people toward strong growth and development in their lives.					
I help persons achieve proactive, constructive behavior in mission.					

Each year affirm the positive reinforcement practices you have well in place. Be in prayer for your personal growth. Live your life with the grace of God.

Positive Reinforcement

With the help of God's grace, develop your positive reinforcement plan for your congregation. Select those positive reinforcement practices that will help your congregation grow forward its generosity.

1. Decide which positive reinforcement practices are already well in place in your congregation. Check these in the column "Well in Place."

2. Select the positive reinforcement practices your congregation can grow forward most easily in year 1. Check these in the column "Year 1."

3. Decide which positive reinforcement practices your congregation can develop best for years 2, 3, and 4. Check in the appropriate column.

	Well in Place	Year 1	Year 2	Year 3	Year 4
We confirm the spirit of generosity and solid creativity in the people around us.					
We share active appreciation for what persons are doing.					
We help people toward strong growth and development in their lives.					
We help persons achieve proactive, constructive behavior in mission.					

Each year affirm the positive reinforcement practices your congregation has well in place. Be in prayer for your congregation. Help your congregation sense well the grace of God.

Advancing Positive Reinforcement—Thank You

With prayer and the help of God's grace, select those "thank-you" practices that will help your congregation grow forward its best generosity.

1. Decide which "thank-you" practices are already well in place in your congregation. Check these in the column "Well in Place."

2. Select the "thank-you" practices you can grow forward most easily in year 1. Check these in the column "Year 1."

3. Decide which "thank-you" practices can be developed best for years 2, 3, and 4. Check in the appropriate column.

	Well in Place	Year 1	Year 2	Year 3	Year 4
Confirmation of pledge/giving					
Increased pledge/giving					
First-time pledge/giving					
New members					
"Thank you" statements					
Recorded contributions "thank you"					
Special gifts "thank you"					
Newsletter/bulletin					
Encouragement letter					
Reports in meetings					
Finance committee meetings					
Year-end "Thank you"					

Each year you positively reinforce the "thank-you" practices you have well in place. Be in prayer for your congregation. Help your congregation sense well the grace of God.

PART FOUR

Stewardship for Giving

Chapter 12

A Grassroots Basis

As you build your understanding of stewardship, I encourage you to develop a *grassroots* understanding of stewardship. Do your best to avoid a focus on the higher-giving households. You will grow the generosity of your congregation more effectively with a focus on the grassroots members.

You can help your congregation build a richer, fuller understanding of stewardship when you focus on:

- the grassroots

- giving

- stewardship.

The grassroots of your congregation includes many of the best potential givers God has given you. In long-range planning, the 20/80 principle is widely used. This principle goes:

> Twenty percent of the things an organization
> does delivers 80 percent of its results.

> Eighty percent of the things an organization
> does delivers 20 percent of its results.

It is sometimes said that 20 percent of the people give 80 percent of the money. This is an interesting extrapolation of the 20/80 principle, but not necessarily accurate.

Some years ago, I became intrigued with whether or not the 20/80 principle could, in fact, be applied to congregational giving. I discovered that in many congregations 30 percent of the people contributed 80 percent of the money. In other congregations 10 percent of the people contributed 90 percent of the money. It is fair to say that we cannot apply the 20/80 principle literally to fund-raising.

It is one thing to know that a relatively small percentage of people give most of the money in many congregations, but another thing to understand why this so often is the case. There are six patterns of giving development contributing to why the 20/80 principle tends to become a self-fulfilling prophecy. And there are ways beyond this imbalance.

First, one reason a large portion of the giving comes from a few people is because the campaign focus is typically on commitment and challenge. These motivational resources resonate well within the small group of the congregation's key leaders, causing this group to respond generously and graciously.

But grassroots members respond to the motivations of compassion and community. An appeal based on commitment and challenge does not spark their generosity. They will give, but not as generously as they are capable of doing. Campaigns focusing on compassion and community inspire much more giving among the grassroots.

Second, we support what we plan. The planning and decision making that shape the annual budget are often done by a select few. It is not surprising that the same select few are the primary financial supporters.

I often hear, "The same few people give most of the money." Closer examination frequently reveals that these same few people are making most of the decisions. Leaders lament, "If they (the grassroots) were more committed, they would give more." This often translates to: "Our small group makes most of the decisions, and we want everyone (the grassroots) to financially support our decisions."

Here is a better way to grow giving forward:

> We want all the grassroots to give generously.
> Therefore, we are including all of them very
> intentionally in the primary decision making.

The advantage of a grassroots long-range planning process is that it broadens the base of decision making and therefore broadens the base of the giving.

A third reason that a few seem to carry the majority of the financial support is that many local churches devote the primary attention in their giving campaigns to the higher-giving households. Many congregations divide their giving campaigns into four divisions: the major gifts division, the advance gifts division, the special gifts division, and the general gifts division. Of these, the first three divisions include only a small percentage, numberwise, of the whole congregation. There is often a certain amount of self-congratulation in this higher-giving group that they "really carry the congregation." The general gifts division, which includes the vast majority of the congregation, is left out of the primary focus.

These things can be changed. You can design your giving campaigns to emphasize and nurture the giving of the grassroots of the congregation, giving them as much focus as the higher-giving households. Many churches are doing precisely that.

There was a time when many individual households within the higher-giving group were not giving at their best. At some point, they were helped to grow forward their giving. Consider what would happen if this same intentional focus were actively shared with grassroots households.

A fourth reason that a few usually give most of the money is because the most competent campaign workers are usually asked to contact the higher-giving households. Wherever you assign your best workers, you are most likely to have your most productive results.

There are many potential major givers among the grassroots. Yet when the most competent workers are not assigned to be in contact with these households, you will seldom discover their giving potential.

Fifth is the way in which the personal invitation to give is shared. In the invitation stage of the campaign, the higher-giving households receive the most time, care, and attention. The personal visits to these members are the most thoughtfully constructive.

Frequently, the higher-giving households are gathered into special small group gatherings in which it is explained to them that their giving is decisive and central to the life of the congregation. Consider what would happen if the same intensity of contact was directed toward the grassroots households.

Sixth, professional campaign fund-raisers tend to focus most on the higher-giving households. There are many excellent fund-raising organizations that perform very helpful services for churches. And yet, some of their fund-raising methodologies focus on the higher-giving households. Their search is for the "big gift." It becomes a self-fulfilling prophecy that a few households will give the biggest proportion of the money.

These six giving development patterns have occurred year after year in many congregations. It is no wonder that for these congregations there are a few who continue to give most of the money. A self-fulfilling prophecy has been operating.

Currently, in your congregation, a small percentage of the people may be giving a large percentage of the money. But this does not mean you have to leave it that way. The situation is not inevitable or predestined.

Share the principles for giving with the grassroots of your congregation—using words of compassion and community—with the same strength, intensity, and creativity as you do with higher-giving households in the congregation. You are successful with these households precisely because you apply effectively with them the principles for giving.

You can grow generous giving in a new group of households in your congregation in these ways:

- Advance the motivations of compassion and community.

- Involve the grassroots in the planning and the key decisions.

- Focus your giving campaigns on the grassroots.

- Select and train your best campaign workers to contact grassroots households.

- Share the personal invitation to give with quality, care, and attention.

- Help your campaign fund-raisers focus on grassroots households.

The generosity of the grassroots will grow.

There is a seventh reason why a few frequently give much of the money: they are being good stewards. The foregoing six reasons focus on and critique the ways campaign leaders, pastors, and fund-raisers frequently relate to higher-giving households. But another reason the few give generously is that they are gracious receivers, good stewards, and want to help. They want their lives to count. They want to grow forward their support of the mission. This is an internal motivation, different from the others, which are external.

Focus on helping both the grassroots and the higher-giving households build a solid understanding of stewardship. Generous giving and solid stewardship go hand in hand.

Chapter 13

════════

Giving

Build stewardship by increasing your understanding of giving. Your understanding of giving directly relates to your philosophy of life. These two, giving and life, are foundational to building a strong sense of stewardship development.

The purpose of stewardship is giving, not fund-raising. How much money can be raised is a secondary objective. The primary purpose of stewardship is to help people learn the art of giving—to grow forward their generosity.

Life is sacred. It is a gift we have received. It is amazing to be alive. The wonders of all the universe do not compare to the gift of life. Life is a treasure—precious and precarious. The riches of life are to be shared. Life at its best is lived through giving, not getting; helping, not hoarding.

Life is for service, not survival; self-giving, not self-serving. People are sometimes scared and scarred, uncertain and insecure. We need to take time to live—to learn to receive and to learn to give.

Giving is not an inherited inclination that some people have and others do not. It is not true that some people are innately givers and some are innately grabbers. Our learnings grow our generosity and our giving.

We are all created in the image and likeness of God. God's nature is amazing grace and generosity. When we live forward to our best true selves, we live forward to generosity and giving. People grow, develop, advance, and build their giving as their learnings teach them of God's, and of others', generosity toward them. Giving is a learned behavior pattern.

People give in direct relation to the ways in which they have experienced giving. People learn generous giving as they experience the generous giving of others and of God. People reflect their experiences.

Giving is more important than fund-raising. Fund-raising is important. Giving is more important. The purpose of stewardship is giving development, not fund-raising. The purpose is to help the givers discover their genuine spirit of generosity.

Regrettably, some have focused too frequently on fund-raising in and of itself. The sad result has been to reduce stewardship to the role of raising a budget. This is a short-sighted, quick-closure, immediate-satisfaction, results-oriented approach that treats the matter solely from the perspective of a fund-raising committee, not a congregation of givers.

When viewed through the eyes of the givers, it is clear that the purpose of stewardship is giving. At its best, stewardship is a service to the giver. It is a resource, not a source of resentment. Unfortunately, some finance committees and some fund-raisers seem to have a "getting-and-grabbing" approach to stewardship. Their attitude teaches people in the congregation a getting-and-grabbing approach to money.

Help persons discover their generosity. When you keep the focus on this, the budget will be raised as a happy by-product, not the central end. The real purpose is to help the giver live life at his or her very best. The purpose is giving development for the sake of the giver, not fund-raising for the sake of the funds.

Gracious receivers become generous givers. The art of stewardship development is to nurture the stages wherein people learn giving:

- Receiving and accepting
- Growing and investing
- Returning and restoring
- Giving and generosity

We can see these stages in the biblical parable of the talents in Matthew 25:14–30. The first stage is receiving and accepting. Three servants received and accepted custody of their master's goods—talents of gold and silver. They could have rejected the money and said, "No, master, I am not worthy to accept these talents." They could have said, "Master, I have all the talents I need."

They could have said, "No, master, I am too busy." They could have debated and discussed the matter among themselves. They could have run the other way. But they didn't. What they did was to receive and accept, not to reject.

The second stage is growing and investing. Two of the servants—one with five talents, one with two talents—went forth, invested, and grew their talents forward. The servant with five talents grew five more. The servant with two talents grew two more. They doubled their money.

The servant with one talent made the mistake of conserving, holding, protecting, and preserving that one talent. This servant buried the talent in the ground so he would not lose it, and his master chastised him.

The third stage is returning and restoring the talents and their increase to the master, not keeping them. The servant with ten talents could have brought back seven and kept three for himself. But he didn't. The servant with four talents could have brought back three talents and kept one for himself. But he didn't.

Both could have rationalized to themselves, "Well, our master will be ahead some and we will be ahead some." What happened was that they returned and restored all they had been given plus all the increase they had grown.

The fourth stage is giving and generosity. The two servants were given yet more talents. The master might have said,

> Thank you very much. Whereas before I possessed
> five talents and two talents, I now have ten talents
> and four talents. Go your own way.

Instead, what the master said was,

> You have been faithful over a little;
> I will make you faithful over much.

God does not hoard what we bring back to Him.

God is seeking to teach us giving and generosity. God graciously receives what we bring back, and then gives and shares yet more generously with us. God is trying to teach us: gracious receivers become generous givers.

Sometimes, we are grabbers and getters. In our haste and hurry to get things for ourselves, we do not receive graciously what God is seeking to give us. Receive graciously what God is giving you. That is the way to a full life.

The key to giving is receiving, for in receiving, we learn how to give. Many people receive generously and graciously, not because of who they are, but of Whose they are. They have received the graciousness and generosity of God's love. Amidst the scaredness and scarredness of life, they have discovered the sacredness and generosity of receiving—and thus of giving.

Learn how to receive. Some people receive ungraciously. They are eager and willing to do many things for other people, but they become awkward and timid when someone wants to give to them. Frequently, they reject the gift because they have not learned how to receive.

Those who give well are those who have learned to receive well. Poor receivers make poor givers. Gracious receivers become generous givers.

Gracious receiving leads to both growing the gifts and restoring them to God. Receiving is not consuming. The servants did not go out and spend the talents. We receive graciously what God gives us. We treat it with trust. We grow and restore to God the gifts with which we have been blessed.

Some giving campaigns miss the receiving, growing, and restoring stages. They focus only on the giving stage because that is what they want people to do—give. When you work with people who are learning how to receive, it does not make sense to push them to the giving stage. That would be putting the cart before the horse. First help them learn how to receive.

Some giving campaigns focus on "what you have been given." This does not grow the art of receiving. Telling people what God has done for them focuses on obligation—"paying back to God" what God has done for us. Rather than teaching people how to receive, this teaches guilt, obligation, and low self-esteem. Reluctant receivers become resentful givers.

Generous giving is more helpful than reluctant giving. To be sure, reluctant giving is still giving, but generous giving is more helpful. God loves a wholehearted and joyous giver—one who gives with gladness and generosity.

Discover the richness of God's grace in your life. Receive the generosity of God's love toward you. Discover best your spirit of generosity and compassion. You will grow forward the generosity and giving in your congregation.

Chapter 14

Stewardship

Stewardship is growing, developing, advancing, and building the gifts with which God has blessed us. Stewardship is not conserving, holding, protecting, and preserving.

God invites you, God calls you to be a good steward of these amazing gifts:

- the gift of your life
- the gift of generosity
- the gift of the mission to which God calls you
- the gift of hope

God encourages you to begin growing, developing, advancing, and building these remarkable gifts.

Regrettably, in some congregations stewardship is portrayed as conserving and holding, protecting and preserving "our meager financial resources." There is no biblical foundation for this. Stewardship is not cautious storing or mindless hoarding. Some who were scared and scarred during the Depression learned from that scarcity to cautiously protect what little they had, and they continue to do so even today. But stewardship is not burying in the ground the gifts God has given us, fearing that we might lose them. God's gifts are meant to be grown and developed.

Stewardship is not putting "our hands in our pockets." In some board meetings, a well-intentioned leader might stand and say,

> We want you to know that we, as good stewards, are doing
> the best we can in these tough times to conserve and hold,
> protect and preserve our church's meager financial resources.

This is not stewardship. Stewardship is not conserving and holding, protecting and preserving.

There are several things that are not accurate in the foregoing statement. Usually, the leaders are not doing their very best. They have not prayed deeply, thought wisely, or acted courageously to advance fully the congregation's giving. More often than not, in a reactive, organizational, passive way, they are simply reporting.

Oddly, in tough times charitable giving advances and increases. Although in affluent times people spend money as though it were going out of style, in tough times, peoples' values center. What is genuinely important in life becomes clearer and dearer.

It is wrong to assume that being a good steward means conserving, holding, protecting, and preserving. It is quite clear in the biblical parable: the servant who sought to conserve, hold, protect, and preserve his one talent was reprimanded; this steward was cast into outer darkness.

It is incorrect to assume that our church has meager financial resources. God supplies resources sufficient to the mission. The dollar not yet given is the dollar not yet asked for.

When a church is without strong financial resources, it is usually a symptom of larger issues related to the relational characteristics of an effective church. Churches almost always think they don't have enough money. They fail to realize that they have all the money they need for God's mission.

The more often someone makes the statement,

> We want you to know that we, as good
> stewards, are doing the best we can in
> these tough times to conserve and hold . . .

the more giving you lose.

Such a statement communicates to the congregation that the best thing they can do is conserve and hold, protect and preserve their own financial resources in these tough times.

Every time the finance committee makes such a statement, the congregation loses money that would otherwise be generously given for the mission. When the finance committee puts its hands in its pockets, it teaches everyone in the congregation to put their hands in their pockets too.

In congregations with a rich, full understanding of stewardship, a wise leader will stand up in a board meeting and say,

God's mission is even more important in these tough times.
We are doing our best to grow, develop, advance, and build
the remarkable gifts with which God is blessing us.

The more frequently this statement is shared, the more money will be given. This statement tells the congregation that the best thing they can do is grow and develop the remarkable gifts with which God has blessed them. When the finance committee takes its hands out of its pockets, it teaches everyone in the congregation to give more generously as well.

When you develop a theology of stewardship as growing, developing, advancing, and building, you live in the confidence that:

- the love of God is renewing

- the power of God is astonishing

- the grace of God is amazing

- the purpose of God is moving

- the hope of God overcomes all.

- Thanks be to God.

People who live with this confidence and vision have a deeply felt, biblical understanding that stewardship is growing the gifts of life, generosity, mission, and hope.

Stewardship is the wise investment of these remarkable gifts. God invites us to increase the harvest of these gifts. God invites us to make wise investments that grow and develop, advance and build the resources with which God has blessed and is blessing us.

The Gift of Life. God invites you to be a steward of the gift of your life. God gives us this one life to live. We can live it richly and fully, or poorly and feebly. God encourages us to live our lives at our best. Life is time, strengths, and future. You are a steward of your life as you are a steward of your time, your strengths, and your future.

God invites us to make wise investments of the time God gives us. Focus on time *investment* as a way to best understand time management. We cannot really manage time. Time moves steadily forward. What we can do is invest wisely to make the best use of the time God gives us. We can live our lives in constructive ways that constitute good investments of our time.

God invites us to make wise investments of the strengths God gives us. When we invest our time, we are also mindful of investing our strengths and competencies. God gives us strengths sufficient unto our mission. God invites us to build on these strengths. God does not want us to become preoccupied with our weaknesses and shortcomings. God will take care of these. We are called to advance the competencies we have been given.

The art of living life lies in claiming our strengths—expanding some of our current strengths and adding new strengths that advance the generosity we can share with those around us. Build on your strengths. Do better what you do best. Then you will be in the strongest position to tackle your weaknesses and shortcomings. Those who begin with their weaknesses are in the weakest position to tackle their weaknesses.

People who claim their strengths claim God's gifts. Those who deny their strengths deny God's gifts. When people are hard on themselves and think more poorly of themselves than they should, when they suffer from low self-esteem, they deny God's gifts—and in this way they deny God.

Those who are good stewards of their lives are the ones who live life through receiving and claiming the strengths and competencies God has given them. The good steward takes his or her current strengths and competencies and grows them forward. The good steward adds new strengths and competencies to those he or she already has well in place.

God invites us to make wise investments of the future that God has given us. When we invest our time and our strengths well, we are investing our future. What is the future toward which you are growing and building, advancing and developing? What are the specific, concrete objectives toward which you are moving?

Objectives are the rudders of life. They give the vital directions to help good stewards make wise investments of their lives. It does not necessarily follow that simply because you have objectives you are therefore a good steward. Choose those objectives that lead you to wisely invest your life.

There is power in priorities. A good steward has some sense of which things in life are priorities. A way to understand the power of priorities is to rank the objectives of your life as A's, B's, C's, and D's.

A's are important and urgent.

B's are important but not urgent.

C's are urgent but not important.

D's are not important and not urgent.

All of us want our lives to count. Our lives count best when we invest our time in the A's and B's.

Solid direction equals strong generosity. Lack of direction equals dependency. When you help people discover the stewardship of their lives—that is, the stewardship of their time, strengths, and future—you help them to advance the generosity of their giving. People who have a sense of their direction and priorities have less need for dependence.

The Gift of Generosity. Just as God invites you to be a good steward of the gift of your life, so God invites you to be a good steward of the gift of generosity. We are created in the image and likeness of God. God's nature is amazing grace and generosity with us. Amidst the sins and alienation of our lives, God gives us the gift of life. God gives us the gift of generosity.

Remember those in your own life who shared the gift of their generosity with you and others around them. The room lit up when they walked in. Their quiet radiance was felt by all. Their easy manner calmed the confusion. Their gentle laughter reassured those around them. They were "someone to whom you could go." They were, simply, generous people.

People who use their time well, build their competencies, and have a sense of direction for their future are in a stronger, more confident position to share the gift of generosity. People who waste their time, play down their strengths, and squander their future are in a weaker position to share the gift of generosity.

God gives each of us the opportunity to share our gift of generosity. We can nurture forward this gift so that it shines in the dark and uplifts all around. We can live with the confidence of being able to share the gift of generosity received from God.

The basis for generosity is to return all to God. That is, invest all that you have grown in ways that advance God's mission. In the parable, the steward who was given five talents and had earned five more returned all ten to the master. The steward who was given two talents and had earned two more returned all of it to his master.

A good steward returns all to the master. As you return all to God, you are freed from thinking you own what you have been given. You are freed from the danger of possessiveness. It is ironic that we sometimes delude ourselves into thinking that we own what we have been given. How can someone own what is a gift?

People who return all to God share well the gift of generosity. They are under no illusion that what they have is theirs. They know all they are and have are God's gifts. They are set free to share generosity.

Receive all of God's gifts, grow forward all of God's gifts, and give all of God's gifts back to God's mission. As you return all to God, you will share the gift of generosity with many people.

The Gift of Mission. God invites you to be a steward of the gift of God's mission. We live in a day of mission. This is not the churched culture of the 1940s and 1950s when it was "the thing to do" to go to church or when many people were seeking out the church on their own initiative and volition. Most of our communities do not reflect the churched culture of busy, bustling suburban churches, with their merry-go-rounds of programs and activities.

This time can best be understood as a rich, full time of mission. In my book *Effective Church Leadership*, this time of mission is fully discussed. There you will discover the foundational life searches important in this life's pilgrimage; the emerging trends of the future; and the ways in which you can grow and develop, advance, and build your leadership competencies as a missionary pastor and mission team leader. Know that one of the gifts God gives to all of us is to be stewards of God's mission.

Being a good steward means far more than simply giving your time, talents, and money to your congregation. Your life counts in extraordinary ways in this time. God has entrusted to us the gift of mission on one of the richest mission fields on the planet.

God invites us to be good stewards of God's mission in two ways:

- to be good stewards with the unchurched
- to be good stewards with the congregation God has given us

See the unchurched as God's gift to us. God invites us to be good stewards with the unchurched. As we are in mission with the unchurched, our lives will count in this time.

In the biblical text, the good shepherd is the one who has ninety-nine sheep in the fold and yet seeks out the one who is lost in the rough, rocky places. It is important to note that the sheep gathered in the fold are actually gathered together in the wilderness. The shepherd gathers the flock in the wilderness, and in that wilderness (in the midst of an unchurched culture), the shepherd seeks the one lost.

Our predicament—indeed, our promise—is that many are lost in the rough, rocky places of life. Congregations that are good shepherd congregations seek out the unchurched in proactive, intentional ways.

Congregations that take as their mission statement the poem "Little Bo Peep" are not good stewards of God's mission. Little Bo Peep has lost her sheep—the unchurched. She doesn't know where to find them. And yet the unchurched are all around, virtually on church doorsteps.

But leave them alone. The myth is that after the young couple has their first child, they will be back in church. Although this happens just enough times to lead us to think this is a reality, it is not. It is a myth. Another myth is that as newcomer families move into our community, they know where we are, let them find us. Just enough newcomer families show up to convince us that this is a reality, but again, it is a myth.

But leave them alone and they'll come home, wagging their tails behind them. The good steward congregation is proactive, relational, missional, and intentional in its outreach with the unchurched. The Bo Peep congregation is like the steward with the one talent or the shepherd who becomes preoccupied with tending the sheep that are left. The Bo Peep congregation is not a good steward of God's mission.

It is important to note that we are good stewards *with* the unchurched, not *for* or *at* the unchurched. Our stewardship in mission with the unchurched is mutual and inclusive, not paternalistic and top-down.

As stewards of God's mission, it is never quite clear who is helping whom. Are we helping the unchurched, or are the unchurched really helping us as we seek to be good stewards? This is what it means for us, as good stewards of God's mission, to be mutually inclusive with the unchurched.

To be a good steward of God's mission is to be a good steward of the congregation with which God has blessed you. God first blesses you with the unchurched, and then God blesses you with your congregation. This order is important and is made quite clear in the New Testament. The text says, "For God so loved the world." The text does not say, "For God so loved the church." God gives us first the mission, and then God gives us the congregation—the outpost, the mission team—with which to be in mission with the unchurched.

In *Twelve Keys to an Effective Church*, I describe the central characteristics that contribute to churches being stable and growing in their mission. Churches that are effective have well in place nine out of the twelve central characteristics. To be a good steward of your congregation is to put well in place the characteristics that:

- match well with the mission field to which God calls you

- match best with the gifts, strengths, and competencies with which God has blessed your congregation.

The concept of wellness and illness is a useful way of understanding the stewardship of a congregation. Those congregations that are putting well in place nine out of the twelve central characteristics are headed toward wellness. Those declining or dying congregations that have barely discovered the unchurched, that have become preoccupied with their own survival, and that are not focusing on the central characteristics they can strengthen are headed toward illness.

When you are a good steward of the congregation with which God has blessed you, you help that congregation toward wellness, to grow beyond a sense of powerlessness, a sense of compulsiveness for perfectionism, a sense of low self-esteem, a sense of depression or dependency, a sense of codependency. You advance that congregation toward healing and wellness. As you do so, you act as a good steward of God's mission.

The Gift of Hope. God invites us to be good stewards of hope. God does not invite us to be custodians of despair, depression, and despondency. God counts on, depends on, yearns for, longs for our being good stewards of hope.

This life's pilgrimage has its share of sinful and tragic events. Amidst all that life brings, people live on hope more than memory. Hope is stronger than memory. Memory is strong. Hope is stronger.

When people cannot see their hopes realized in the present, they postpone their hopes "down the road" into the future. When they cannot foresee their hopes being realized in the immediate future, they postpone their hopes to the distant future. And when they cannot foresee their hopes being realized in the immediate or distant future, they postpone their hopes to the next-life future—"beyond the river." They become what I affectionately call "the river people."

We become river people when we vest our hopes in the next life—beyond the river. When we do this, we are not being good stewards of hope. We know two things to be true about the Kingdom:

First, the Kingdom is now here, now there. It reveals itself in every event of reconciliation, wholeness, caring, and justice. In every event of hope, there the Kingdom happens.

Second, the Kingdom is not yet in its fullness.

It is not appropriate that we vest all our hopes in the next life. Some of our hopes will be realized in this life as we serve in mission.

Sometimes we become the flimsies people. We vest our hopes in the "fleeting flimsies" of this life—a new car, new clothes, new equipment. Our search for hope is sufficiently desperate that we cannot see hope in the present, the immediate, or distant future. We do not even see hope beyond the river. When we feel cut off from all of these sources of hope, we move from one fleeting flimsy moment to the next, seeking solace in the material things of this life.

The problem of our time is primarily a vacuum of hope, not a focus on materialism. People invest their hopes in material things not because they think there is something enduring in them but because they are looking for hope—even when it is fleeting, flimsy, and momentary.

Sometimes we become the cliff people. Mountain climbers sometimes find themselves on the face of a cliff, unable to see any handholds or footholds backward or forward. What people tend to do in such a precarious predicament, whether on the face of the cliff or at other difficult times in life, is to freeze—to clutch and cling for dear life. Frozen in that position, we want no change, because the only change we can see is the abyss below.

Some of us are frozen and fearful in our lives. We cannot help these fearful people by shouting down instructions from the safety of the cliff top. What we need to do is join the person on the face of the cliff. Gently, softly, slowly, we can coach the cliff person to the next handhold, then the next foothold. We can help them find handles of hope.

Through the gift of His Son, God invites us forward to be the Easter people. God invites us to be the people of hope. God gives to us the gift of hope, that we might be good stewards of that gift—that we might nourish it, help it to grow, develop, advance, and build. God invites us to be the stewards of this enduring, inviting, compassionate hope so that people around us—so that you and I—can discover rich full glimpses of hope. We discover glimpses of hope, now here and now there, in which God acts with reconciliation, wholeness, caring, and justice. In those events, the Kingdom happens. In those events, hope is richly present.

Build your understanding of stewardship. Be a good steward of the gift of life, the gift of generosity, the gift of mission, and the gift of hope. These are God's gifts with you. Help your family, your friends, the people with whom you are in mission, and your congregation to grow these gifts as well.

PERSONAL GROWTH ACTION WORKSHEET

Building your Stewardship Gifts

1. Decide which stewardship gifts are already well in place in your life. Check these in the column "Well in Place."

2. Select the gifts you can grow forward most easily in year 1. Check in the column "Year 1."

3. Decide which gifts can be developed best for years 2, 3, and 4. Check in the appropriate column.

	Well in Place	Year 1	Year 2	Year 3	Year 4
I will grow the gift of Life, which God has given me.					
I will develop the gift of Generosity with those around me.					
I will advance the gift of Mission with my life and my congregation.					
I will build the gift of Hope in my life and in the lives of those I seek to serve.					

Each year positively reinforce the stewardship gifts you have well in place. Be much in prayer for your own growth in stewardship and for those with whom you are growing.

Building the Stewardship Gifts of Your Congregation

1. Decide which of these stewardship gifts are already well in place in your congregation. Check these in the column "Well in Place."

2. Select the gifts you can grow forward most easily in your congregation in year 1. Check these in the column "Year 1."

3. Decide which gifts can be developed best for years 2, 3, and 4. Check in the appropriate column.

	Well in Place	Year 1	Year 2	Year 3	Year 4
We will grow the gifts of Life, which God has given our congregation.					
We will develop the gift of Generosity with those in our congregation and with those with whom we are serving.					
We will advance the gift of Mission in our congregation and in the world.					
We will build the gift of Hope in our congregation and in the lives of those we seek to serve.					

Each year positively reinforce the stewardship gifts your congregation has well in place. Be much in prayer for your congregation's growth in stewardship and for those with whom you are growing.

Conclusion

Chapter 15

Money for Mission

Giving and living are for mission—and money is for mission. We give ourselves, our lives, and our money to advance God's mission in these decisive times. Our values center on mission.

Values are taught. Giving values and living values are taught by you and your congregation. Likewise, money values are taught by the way your congregation focuses on money.

We have all learned attitudes, values, and behavior patterns in relation to money. In our early years we learned these values in our family. Growing up, we learned these values in our peer groups. As adults, we continue to learn these values from the significant relational groups important in our lives.

One of these groups is the congregation in which you have found roots, place, and belonging, a sense of family and community. In this environment we continue to learn attitudes, values, and behavior patterns in relation to money. These learnings shape in important ways how we deal with money in our families, in our work, in our own identity and personhood, in our lives, and in our life's mission.

In some congregations, people learn that money is a preoccupation. For some congregations, the primary goal is that the budget must balance at the end of the year. I agree that it is a good thing to have the budget balance. However, when balancing the budget becomes a preoccupation, the value system becomes warped.

In some congregations, being a leader is equated with being a manager of money. The focus is: "We must manage our money carefully so that the budget balances at the end of the year." This causes key leaders, finance committees, and pastors to focus primarily on policies, procedures, rules, and regulations, because they are relating primarily to money. This preoccupation teaches people in the congregation that it is acceptable in this life's pilgrimage to be preoccupied with money.

Our culture is already obsessed enough with money. Perhaps a congregation's preoccupation with money is learned from the culture. When a church becomes obsessed with money, it teaches and reinforces this preoccupation in its members. This attitude does not advance personal growth and development, nor does it advance the generosity of people's giving.

In some congregations, people are taught the value that money is power. There are a few people on finance committees and a few pastors who use their control of the budget as a way to gain control of the church. Instead of seeking to advance the church's mission, they seek to achieve control and power.

In this perspective, the leader is the boss, the authoritative dictator, who controls the money. Some people presume that one way to be the boss in a local church is to control the money. Such a controlling approach does not advance the generosity of people's giving. In a mission congregation, the leaders of the mission are the ones who have the power. They are the ones who give leadership to the congregation's present and future mission.

In some congregations, people learn the value that money is a necessary evil. This is particularly true of congregations in which the leader is a charismatic inspirer who focuses on apocalyptic events. For these congregations, inspiration is at its best when the apocalypse is at its worst.

In these congregations, the failure to raise enough money for the budget is a sign of the sinfulness of the congregation. It is an indication that the congregation lacks commitment. Although money itself is considered sinful, it is a necessary evil that will help the church move beyond the present crisis. Such congregations are taught the attitude, value, and behavior pattern that money is evil.

This approach frequently causes families to teach children that money is sinful. We need it, but we don't like the fact that we need it. We can't get along without it, but at the same time, we wish we could. This negative approach to money does not advance the generosity of people's giving.

In the Bible, we discover these words:

> For the love of money is a root of all sorts of evil, and some
> by longing for it have wandered away from the faith.
>
> *1 Tim. 6:10*

It is the love and longing that is a root of all sorts of evil, not the money itself. The love of money tends to fill the vacuum left by the absence of a longing to serve God's mission.

Money is for mission. When a congregation is immersed in God's mission, its longing is to serve God. When this love and longing are kept central, it is difficult for the love of and longing for money to find a way in. When you and I are immersed in God's mission, our longings are to serve God. When this love and longing are kept central, it is difficult for the love and longing of money to find a way into our lives.

In many congregations, people learn the positive, constructive value that money helps mission. Money is not an end in itself. It is helpful to advance God's mission.

Mission leaders understand the relative value of money. They do not make money a preoccupation. They do not quest after power, nor do they turn money into a necessary evil. Money is simply an effective, helpful means to advance God's mission—one among many constructive means.

This understanding of money helps families to not be preoccupied with money, to not see money as power, to not see money as sinful. Yes, money is helpful with food, clothing, shelter. Money helps with life's necessities and with life's enjoyments. To what end? To serve God's mission.

Life is mission. Each of us is called to discover our life mission. Food, clothing, and shelter are not ends in themselves; they serve the mission. The necessities and enjoyments of life are shared in the light of the mission to which God calls us.

This understanding creates people who see money as a simple, constructive means to advance their lives as individuals and as families, and to advance God's mission in the world. The way in which people value money affects their giving and their living. The way in which people understand giving and stewardship affects the way they value money. Money is for mission.

Each part of this book has shared one of the steps that will help you grow and develop your giving and your living. Do the four steps well—in your own life and in your congregation.

- Grow the principles for giving.

- Develop the possibilities for giving.

- Advance the motivations for giving.

- Build your understanding of stewardship.

Be a gracious receiver and a generous giver. Be a good steward of God's gifts—life, generosity, mission, hope. You will grow your own generosity and the generosity of your congregation. God bless you. God be with you.